HOW TO WRITE FOR PUBLICATION

In this series:

WRITE FOR PUBLICATION

The professional author's handbook

Second Edition

Chriss McCallum

How To Books

Cataloguing in publication data
A catalogue record for this book is available from the British Library

© Copyright 1989 and 1992 by Chriss McCallum

Consultant Editor: Roland Seymour

First published in the UK in 1989. Fully revised second edition published in 1992 by
How To Books Ltd, Plymbridge House,
Estover Road, Plymouth PL6 7PZ, United Kingdom.
Tel: Plymouth (0752) 735251. Fax: (0752) 695699. Telex: 45635.

Typeset by Kestrel Data, Exeter
Printed and bound in Great Britain by
The Cromwell Press Limited, Melksham, Wiltshire

Contents

List of Illustrations

Foreword to The Second Edition

My delight at being invited to write a foreword to this book is tempered only by the fact that it really doesn't need one. Just glance at the list of contents or flick through the pages at random and you'll quickly realise that here is a general guide for the writer—and particularly the novice writer—as valuable as the Highway Code is to the motorist.

Totally free of waffle; packed with good, solid advice and information; entertaining, instructional *and* encouraging all at the same time. A really excellent choice as a 'starter' book for any aspiring writer and a more than useful addition to the shelves of even the most professional one. It is, quite simply, one of the best books of its kind that I've ever read.

Steve Wetton
Author of BBC TV's comedy-drama *Growing Pains*

Preface

You want to write, and you want to get your writing published. Where do you start?

THINGS YOU NEED TO KNOW

- What to write
- How to write it
- Where and how to sell it.

You need a guide

It's a bit of a maze, this writing business. You'll be surprised how big it is, too. It's no use wandering about on your own. You'll only waste time and effort—and money.

Try to resist the itch to pick up a pen or plug in your keyboard till you've taken the round trip. You'll be ready then to decide which point of entry you want to try first.

Feedback from the first edition and from writers who responded to our 1991 questionnaire tells us that fiction writing is the most popular of all the writing fields. To reflect this interest and to help fiction writers achieve success, this new edition includes detailed constructive advice on revising and editing your own work. Don't disregard the other options, though. There's ten times more non-fiction than fiction published today, and there's no reason why you shouldn't write both.

Acknowledgements

For permission to publish original quotes, copyright material and personal experiences, the author and publishers thank Alan Bond, Patricia Brennan, Wally K. Daly, J.T. Edson, Peter Finch, Robert Goddard, Robbie Gray, Diann Greenhow, Paul Heapy, Joan B. Howes, Ted Hughes, H.R.F. Keating, Joyce Lister, Brian Lumley, Dorothy Lumley, Harry Mulholland, Mike Pattinson, Peggy

Poole, Ken Rock, Pat Saunders, Jean Sergeant, Liz Taylor, Graham Thomas, D.C. Thomson & Co Ltd, Gordon Wells, Steve Wetton and Charles R. Wickins.

Author's Note
Editors and publishers, like writers, spring from both sexes. If anyone can invent a workable device to convey that fact neatly and without the awkward use of 'he and she', 'he/she', '(s)he' and suchlike, I'll be glad if you'll send it on. In the meantime, please read 'he', 'him' and 'his' throughout the text as embracing both men and women. Ne sexism is intended—after all, despite my slightly androgynous name, I am a woman.

1
Getting Started

BEFORE YOU STEP IN

To be a writer, all you have to do is apply your pen to paper, and let the words flow out. Writing for the sheer pleasure of expressing your thoughts and feelings is a very satisfying activity.

But it isn't satisfying enough for *you*, is it? You don't just want to be a writer—you want to be a *published* writer.

There are no foolproof methods. There are no absolute rules. You can write anything you like. To get your work into print, however, there's one fact of life you can't afford to ignore: writing for publication is a hard-headed and fiercely competitive business. If you accept that at the outset, you'll approach your writing and the business of selling it in the best way and with the best chance of success.

It's a buyer's market. Don't underestimate what that means. The acceptance rate for unsolicited book manuscripts, for instance, is about one in two thousand—very long odds. But you *can* shorten them. You can:

● Get to know how the publishing business works.
● Learn how to identify, analyse and approach your markets.
● Understand why you have to offer editors what they want, not what you think they *should* want.
● Learn how to develop a mutually profitable professional relationship with the editors you want to do business with.

The writing world is full of hopeful authors who will never see a word of theirs in print, because they don't—or won't—understand that they have to study and work at both the craft of writing and the art of selling.

First serve your apprenticeship

There's no secret recipe, no magic formula for success. Tedious it might sound, but the only way to succeed is to *work*. Writing is a creative art, yes, but the art can only be developed from a sound knowledge of the craft. You would never dream, would you, of getting up on a public platform to play the piano if you didn't know one note from another? Yet legions of writers bombard editorial offices with manuscripts that are unstructured, badly written and all too often directed to the wrong publisher anyway. These writers are constantly amazed and upset because their manuscripts boomerang home trailing rejection slips.

You don't have to court such disappointment. You can take the time and trouble to learn:

- the **basic techniques** of good writing
- how to **structure** your writing
- how to **choose and use language** to the best possible effect
- how to **communicate your thoughts** without muddle or ambiguity
- how to **capture and hold your reader's interest**
- how to **revise and rewrite**, and rewrite again until you're sure the work is as good as you can make it.

Throughout this book you'll find references to books and magazines, courses, associations, services and information sources that will help you to master the craft of writing and develop the skills you need to succeed in getting your work published. To avoid unnecessary repetition, you'll find the full details in the appendices —names, addresses, telephone numbers, and prices and subscription/membership rates where applicable.

You'll also read words of wisdom, encouragement and occasionally caution, from editors and from published writers, some of whom are just at the beginning of their career but many of whom are well established and well known. You don't have to agree with them—they don't always agree with each other—but what they have to say is well worth reading. These are people who know the business. They want to help you to know it too.

Take yourself seriously

It isn't easy to think of yourself as a serious writer when you're just starting out. You're probably worried about your chances of success, and nagged by doubts that wake you up in the small hours. Maybe you're worried because you can't make up your mind about what kind of writing is right for you. Don't worry. Most writers feel like this at first—and those who are too sure of themselves tend to trip over their own egos. Have confidence in your own capacity to learn. Approach your writing from the beginning in a professional manner. After all, if you don't believe in your potential ability, how can you expect to convince others?

> As I myself found, one of the biggest deterrents at the beginning of a writing career is the inability to take yourself seriously. It seems as if you are yearning after an impossible dream, seeking to enter a world inhabited by the greats. It is difficult to realise that most other writers have started with the same doubts and uncertainties.
>
> Liz Taylor, *The Writing Business*

And be taken seriously

The first part of the book is designed to help you build your credibility. It will give you a working knowledge of the business of writing and its accepted practices and conventions, so that you can avoid many of the pitfalls that commonly beset the in-experienced writer.

This knowledge will also equip you to decide more easily where you want to start, and you'll get far more out of the information in the second part. Even if you've already chosen your field (or if your field has chosen you, as often happens), don't disregard the other options altogether. You might want to branch out later on.

Common sense

Many beginner writers seem to be drawn to one or the other of two extreme attitudes. First, there's the new writer who devours all the advice he can lay hands on, and who treats every word as gospel. He then gets himself in a terrible twist, endlessly trying to adapt his style, his approach, his technique, his marketing strategy, because the writers' magazine or manual he's reading this week contradicts the advice in the one he read last week. He has no faith at all in his own judgement, and gives himself no chance to develop any.

Then there's the opposite type, the beginner who refuses to consider *any* advice or help from anyone. He drives editors to distraction by disregarding even the most basic common-sense principles. He's the one who shoots off book-length stories to tiny magazines, single poems to book publishers, erudite essays to mass-market magazines . . .

Neither of these writers uses his common sense. The result is that they create problems where none existed before.

This book aims to show you the practical, common-sense ways to succeed in getting your work published. Above all, it will enable you to develop reliance on your own judgement, based on the information you'll read here and in the recommended books, and then on the experience you'll gradually acquire for yourself.

Here, then, are a few basic common-sense *DOs* and *DON'Ts* to bear in mind as you read:

1. *Do* study the techniques of good, clear writing, but *don't* submerge your individual instincts.
2. *Do* study your markets to make sure the material you send them is suitable, but *don't* carbon-copy the style and content so closely that you sacrifice every trace of originality.
3. *Do* be courteous and businesslike in all your dealings with editors, but *don't* regard them either as enemies or gods. They're not 'anti' new writers, or unapproachable, or infallible, or exalted—they're human beings with problems and prejudices, mortgages and falling hair, just like the rest of us.
4. *Do* work at cultivating your own judgement, but *don't* attempt to defy the conventions before you understand them.
5. And, above all, *do* write. *Don't* just think or talk or read or dream about writing. *Do it.*

HOW TO GET STARTED

In theory, all you need is a pen and a pad of paper. In practice, it isn't that simple. Editors won't read hand-written scripts. You need to be able to present your work in the form of a **typescript**. Though it looks like a contradiction in terms, this is usually called a **manuscript** (abbreviation 'ms', plural 'mss').

You'll save a lot of money if you can type your ms yourself. Current rates for a professionally typed ms are upwards of £3 per 1,000 words plus extra for copies (and you need at least one complete copy). A 60,000 word novel, then, could cost about £200 just for typing, more than the price of many good quality electronic typewriters. Even two or three short stories could cost you nearly as much as buying a small portable.

It isn't difficult to learn. There are short courses and evening classes, or you could teach yourself with a simple manual like Brenda Rowe's *Type It Yourself.*

BASIC EQUIPMENT

You need pens, and small notebooks you can carry in your pocket or bag, to note *anything* that might be useful. If you can afford one, a pocket tape recorder is even better. Ideas, words, phrases, overheard anecdotes can slip away forever if you don't note them down somehow at the time.

Students' A4 lined notepads are popular with writers who write their first drafts in longhand. Others prefer to work straight on to a typewriter or word processor. Whichever method you choose, you'll eventually need the following to market your writing:

- If you work on a word processor, a decent letter-quality printer. Most editors dislike dot matrix printers. Some, especially in the USA, refuse to read work produced on them.

- For typewritten mss, plain white A4 bond paper for top copies. (Don't waste it on notes or drafts—anything will do for those. Save unwanted flyers, defunct letters and the like.)

- A4 bank paper, for carbon copies. Use coloured bank for your own file copies if you like, but don't send coloured mss to editors.

- Black A4 carbon paper.

- Black typewriter ribbons. Don't economise on these—replace them before they run out.

- Plain white business envelopes, 9 x 4½ ins.

- 'Giant' manilla envelopes, 9 x 6½ ins, to hold A4 sheets folded once.

- A4 manilla envelopes, to send without folding mss of more than about six sheets.

Office supply shops are cheaper than high street stationers for paper and envelopes. Shop around and compare prices. If your typing is good, you could use A4 plain white copier paper, which is perfectly acceptable for mss, but which doesn't erase as well as bond. Ask for 80 gsm (grammes per square metre) weight plain copier paper—it's half the price of bond. Make friends with your local office supplier. He might agree to a small discount if you undertake to buy all your stationery supplies there.

Do you need a word processor?

No, you don't. If you have one already, then of course you'll use it, but if you don't, then don't rush out and buy one on the strength of anticipated earnings from your writing. A word processor is a sophisticated and very useful tool, but it isn't a writer. Don't make the mistake of thinking that any tool will magically produce publishable work. Nothing and no one can do the creating but you.

Every successful writer works in his or her own way. Russell Hoban said during a Writers-on-Tour seminar that it took him four years to master his Apple II, but now he would never work any other way. (He even gave his Apple a starring role in his novel *The Medusa Frequency*.) But Fay Weldon, interviewed on Channel Four, declared that if the day ever comes when she's required to write on a machine, she'll stop writing. She writes with a pen and pad, and pays someone else to type her mss.

A useful book for word processor enthusiasts is *The Writer and the Word Processor* by Ray Hammond.

USEFUL BOOKS

Buy these books if you can—you'll use them a lot:

● A big fat dictionary. *Chambers 20th Century* is a good one.

● An up-to-date copy of the *Writers' & Artists' Yearbook*, an annual directory of book, magazine and newspaper publishers, with names, addresses and telephone numbers and information about what they publish. It also gives sound advice about writing and publishing, agents, associations, services, taxation liabilities, rights, copyright and so on.

● *The Oxford Dictionary for Writers and Editors*. Very useful for checking difficult spellings and usage, including lots of proper names, capitalisation, abbreviations, foreign words and phrases.

- *Research for Writers* by Ann Hoffmann, a comprehensive reference book for finding information sources.

- A concise encyclopedia, like the annual *Pears Cyclopedia*.

- *Roget's Thesaurus*, which lists synonyms for almost every word in the English language. Marvellous for finding just the right word—but don't get addicted to it.

- *The Writer's Handbook*, a writers' directory which appeared for the first time in 1988. The only current rival to the *Writers' & Artists' Yearbook*, it doesn't list as many outlets as the *Yearbook* but gives more detailed information about those it does include, and covers more radio, TV and stage outlets. Use it as a complement to the *Yearbook* rather than a substitute.

Books about writing
There are dozens of books to show you how to write publishable work. You'll find details of books about writing for specific fields in the appropriate sections later in the book. The books listed here are recommended especially for new writers who want to familiarise themselves with the practice and business of writing.

- *An Author's Guide to Publishing* by Michael Legat. Lots of information about book publishing, contracts, presentation, author-publisher relations.
- *Writing for Pleasure and Profit* by Michael Legat. Very readable coverage of many fields of writing, and particularly good on novels.
- *The Writing Business* by Liz Taylor. Enthusiastic, encouraging and practical—rich in insights into the writer's world and work.
- *Writing Step by Step* by Jean Saunders. A clear and concise guide designed for beginning writers, looking at the various choices available.
- *The Successful Author's Handbook* by Gordon Wells. Thoroughly practical, down-to-earth guide to writing for the non-fiction markets.
- *The Way to Write* by John Fairfax and John Moat. The originators of the Arvon Foundation explain the basic techniques of good writing.

FINDING WHAT YOU NEED

Library services

The public library should be able to get *any* book that's in print for you, and many that are out of print, from other libraries in your district or from the Inter-Library Loan Service which operates through the British Lending Library. This might involve a small charge (usually under £1). Your library will advise you.

As you'll probably be using the library a good deal, it's worth making a note of the main category divisions of the Dewey Decimal Classification System, which is used in most UK libraries. The category numbers are shown on the shelves, and it saves time if you know where to start looking:

000	General Works	500	Science
100	Philosophy	600	Technology
200	Religion	700	The Arts and Recreations
300	Social Sciences	800	Literature
400	Languages	900	Geography, Biography and History

Out of print books and books on your special subjects

The monthly *Book and Magazine Collector* lists books for sale and wanted, together with articles and information about collectable authors and illustrators and their works. Although it's primarily intended for book dealers and collectors, it's useful for writers, too. Many dealers specialise, and you can ask those who specialise in your own fields of interest to put you on their mailing lists. Or you can advertise for books yourself. The *Book and Magazine Collector* also carries advertisements for book-finding services, that is, dealers who will find particular books for you through their contacts in the business.

Writers' magazines

There are a few magazines specially produced for writers. They print advice, news, reviews, competition notices and other information on what's happening on the writing scene, plus articles by writers discussing the craft and business of writing.

Quartos, a bi-monthly A4 production of 24 pages, is an excellent source of information about writing competitions, and also carries articles, comment columns, news, reviews, and market information.

Freelance Writing and Photography is a 32-page A4 quarterly, packed with news and information. This long-established magazine has found a stable home with Weavers Press, under the editorship of John T. Wilson, after a few years of uncertainty about style, content and ownership.

Writers' Own Magazine and *The Writer's Rostrum* are quarterly A5 magazines carrying articles about writers and writing, and publishing their readers' poetry and short stories. Both are very friendly and encouraging to new writers.

Writer's Monthly is a glossy A4 magazine published by the company which runs The Writing School. It carries articles on writers and writing, many of which are contributed by well-known writers in various fields, as well as market news, advice and information.

Writers News is another glossy production in A4 format, published by David St John Thomas, former owner of David and Charles Publishers. A monthly publication carrying a good deal of news snippets about markets, competitions and so on, its content, in the main, is written by regular contributors.

The Author and *The Writers' Newsletter* are, respectively, the official magazines of The Society of Authors and The Writers' Guild of Great Britain. Non-members can buy them on subscription.

Finding photographs

If you need photographs to illustrate your book you'll find a list of photographic agencies and picture libraries in the *Writers' & Artists' Yearbook*. One of the largest agencies is Popperfoto (Paul Popper Ltd), whose commercially available visual material amounts to a staggering 15,000,000 illustrations. Popperfoto lend their material worldwide, usually on a same-day basis, for reproduction purposes. It's mainly publishers who use these services, but a private individual can use them too. However, the costs are quite high, and there's a service fee payable whether you use the illustrations or not. The use of a single black and white photograph, with UK rights only, could cost from around £30 upwards plus the service charge. Mrs Liz Moore, manager of Popperfoto, always advises authors:

- not to start researching pictures till you have a publisher;
- wherever possible leave the research to the publisher—they know far more about it than authors;

- make sure you have it in writing that the publisher will be responsible for payments and for the safekeeping of the photos, otherwise *you* might be charged for any damage.

There's an excellent book on the subject, *The Art of Picture Research* by Hilary Evans. You can buy the book through booksellers or direct from Mr Evans. See under Books for Writers in Further Reading, page 179.

Your local photographic society
There are probably quite a few members of your local photographic society who would be delighted to supply you with photographs. You could come to an arrangement about making payment if and when your material is published, and give an undertaking that the photographer's work will be credited to him.

Free photographs
Many large industrial and commercial companies will allow you to use photographs of their products and related items free of charge, provided you give the company due acknowledgement and therefore publicity.

If there's a company whose products and/or services might be suitable as illustrations for your book or article, it's worth contacting their publicity officer to ask about this.

You could also try enquiring at tourist information centres. Some of these will supply free slides or prints to accompany material that promotes their area.

Take your own
If you need some guidance on how to take your own photographs to complement your writing, read Gordon Wells's first-class book *Photography for Article-Writers*, recently published in the Allison & Busby Writers' Guides series. Thoroughly practical, it covers every possible aspect of taking saleable pictures, from camera choice through composition and processing to presentation and keeping records. What kind of photos to take—and what not to take—and how to marry your writing and your photographs: everything you need to know is here.

INSPIRATION, SUPPORT AND TUITION

Writing can be a lonely business. Some writers prefer to work alone, but others need the stimulation of company, to spark off ideas and exchange thoughts and views (and complaints about editors and agents). Once you start looking for kindred spirits, you'll be surprised how many there are around you.

Writers' groups

There might be a writers' group already meeting in your district, or at least close enough for you to attend occasionally. Your library will have contact names and addresses.

You can get a *Directory of Writers' Circles*, compiled by Jill Dick, which lists contact names and addresses throughout the UK. Details are in the appendices, under Useful Booklets in Further Reading.

If there isn't a group near you, why not start one yourself? A notice in your local paper (contact the editor) or pinned up in the library could turn up at least one or two fellow scribes. You can meet once or twice a month in each other's homes, or just meet occasionally but keep in touch by telephone. With enough members, you could hire a room regularly and share the cost.

'Is this where they write Spitting Image, Engelbert?'

Meeting other writers in a group can help in several ways. A group is mutually supportive, providing encouragement and comfort. As well as discussing work and problems, you can share the cost of subscriptions to writers' magazines, and build up a library of writers' manuals and reference books. Each member can contribute magazines to a market study collection, and you could club together to buy stationery in bulk. Your local Arts Council office will advise you about inviting guest speakers, and will help you to find them. Some Regional Arts Boards have schemes which help groups to pay for guest speakers.

Postal workshops
Sometimes called 'folios', postal workshops are systems where writers circulate their work-in-progress around a limited number of other workshop members. Each member contributes comments on the other members' work before passing the folio on to the next member. Each workshop usually concentrates on a specific genre of writing—writing for children, novel-writing, writing for radio and so on.

Catherine Gill has recently launched a *Directory of Postal Workshops*, which will be continually updated, and will send you a copy at a charge of £1 post free. The postal workshop system is particularly useful for writers who find it difficult to get to writing classes or meetings of writers' groups.

Classes, seminars and residential courses
Most **Local Education Authority (LEA)** and **Workers' Educational Association (WEA)** courses include some on creative writing and related subjects. These are usually advertised in the local press before the start of each term, and your library should have information.

Seminars and **courses** are held all over the country and all through the year. As you become familiar with the writer's world, and begin to receive the information that comes in and with writers' magazines, you'll find a wide range of events you can take part in.

Writers who get involved in seminars and residential courses find that their enthusiasm and enjoyment carries over into writing at home, and keeps them going when they might otherwise become discouraged. This inspiration and encouragement is evident to the tutors as well as their students. Ted Hughes, the Poet Laureate, takes an active part in the Arvon Foundation, and is enthusiastic in his support of the courses:

On a good course, the excitement and delight of the students has to be seen to be believed. And no one would credit the transformation it works on many of them, unless he had seen it. The whole course is designed to achieve this result, and nine times out of ten it does achieve it. The tutors want it to happen, and the students want it to happen, so it happens.

Ted Hughes, the Poet Laureate

The **Arvon Foundation** offers residential courses at its two centres, Lumb Bank in Yorkshire and Totleigh Barton in Devon. Five-day courses include board, lodging and tuition—current prices on application. Reductions are available to the low-waged, unemployed, students and pensioners. There are facilities for physically disabled people. The course tutors include some of the best-known writers in the country, like P.D. James and Stan Barstow. You can get full details of current and projected courses on request.

The **Writers' Summer School**, Swanwick, is a six-day annual event. This is the oldest established of the writers' conferences, having begun in 1949. There are about 300 places, but it's usually oversubscribed so you should apply early. The conference is held in August, and attracts top writers as tutors and speakers. Details and application form sent on request.

Scarborough Writers' Weekend has been an annual event since 1973, usually in April. This is a wonderfully stimulating and enjoyable event, with a wealth of workshops and discussions, and top speakers.

Caerleon Writers' Holiday, a week-long gathering of writers held each summer. There's a packed programme of workshops, tutorials, talks and seminars. The 1992 programme introduces 'hands-on' tuition in word-processing in addition to the usual activities.

The **National Institute of Adult Continuing Education (NIACE)** issues a comprehensive handbook every six months, giving the half-year's list of residential short courses held at various locations. NIACE will send you the handbook for a small charge—it lists many creative writing courses.

Network Scotland Limited supplies information on creative writing courses throughout Scotland, as well as information leading to qualifications in literature and journalism. Each enquiry is dealt with as it comes, as the information is extensive and changes frequently. You can enquire by phone or letter, or drop in personally. Network Scotland will also send you a leaflet about their **education information services**.

London Media Workshops run workshops and courses on writing for radio, TV, video and the press. The tutors are drawn from the top people working in these media. You can have your name put on the mailing list for **workshops information** and the **postal books service**, which includes many writers' manuals.

Contact your Regional Arts Board

Ask the office of your nearest **Regional Arts Board**—your library will have the address, or look it up in the *Writers' & Artists' Yearbook*—to put your name on their regular mailing list of literary events: Writers-on-Tour, readings, workshops, information about material, including books, published locally. (Local publishers are often interested in work by local writers.) You'll also receive information about **arts festivals**, where you can make contact with other writers, and possibly have the opportunity to read your own work.

Correspondence courses

The value of correspondence courses is the subject of on-going debate. One writers' magazine conducted a survey among its readers and found that success or failure appeared to depend almost entirely on the calibre of the tutors. The response from course students, past and current, also indicated that the chances of a student being allocated a competent and helpful tutor are no more than 50-50. It appears, too, that in most cases the only qualification needed to become a tutor is to be 'a published writer'—of what and how long ago doesn't seem to be an issue. When you consider the high cost to the student, this is not encouraging. Success, then, would appear to be as much a matter of luck as of hard work on the student's part.

The only courses that attracted no negative comments in the survey were those offered by the **London School of Journalism**.

If you're interested in such a course, you'll find prominent advertising by the bigger schools in the national press. There are also specialist courses on writing for children and on writing technical material—see the appropriate chapters.

'Written By' is a new course recently launched by two of our top scriptwriters, Vince Powell and George Evans. Following the BBC radio series *Get Writing* and the publication of their book of the same name, Vince and George decided to offer their own experience and expertise to help aspiring writers. The big difference between 'Written By' and other correspondence courses is that Vince and George do all the tutoring themselves— no outside tutors are employed. And with credits like *Coronation Street, Never the Twain, Blind Date, Up Pompeii*, as well as numerous screenplays, books and articles, there's a wealth of experience here. And there's no 'farming out'. There's a complete multi-media course (currently £240), but you can specialise if you prefer, at proportionate charges. Details and costs on request.

And a place for work
The London Writing Rooms will rent rooms to writers. For under £40 per week you can rent a private room, 24 hours a day, 365 days a year, with your own key, the use of a kitchen, and a telephone for out-going calls only. If you can interest fellow writers who live within reach of London, you might think about organising a 'time-share' letting.

CHECKLIST

Start drawing up a plan of action. Here are a few basic first steps—you can add to them as your knowledge grows and your ambitions begin to focus.

Objective	How to achieve it
1. Begin to learn about the writing business.	Buy, or borrow from the library, *Writing for Pleasure and Profit* (Michael Legat) and *The Writing Business* (Liz Taylor).
2. If you can't already type, take action to learn.	Buy or borrow a reasonably good machine. Buy a typing manual or arrange tuition.
3. Join (or initiate) a writers' group.	Make enquiries at the library. Advertise for other writers to make contact.
4. Begin to get to know the pleasures and problems you'll have in common with other writers, both new and experienced.	Send for a copy of at least one writers' magazine.

5. Start to whet your appetite for eventual publication.

Buy and read through the *Writers' & Artists' Yearbook* or *The Writer's Handbook*—both, if you can.

KEEPING RECORDS

To keep your writing affairs in order, it's best to start making simple records right at the beginning. Note everything down as it happens. If you leave it till the end of the month—or even the end of the week—you'll probably forget something. You need the following:

1. A **cash book**, to record expenditure. Note every penny spent, including the purchase of this book, and keep the receipts in a file. Note, too, any money you earn from your writing, no matter how small the sum.
2. A **record book**, to keep track of your articles, stories, poems— where you send them, whether they're accepted or rejected, paid for or not and so on.
3. A **markets book**, to record your dealings with individual markets. Keep detailed notes as you gather information and experience of each one. List every item you send there, and keep a record of its progress. Note how you found that market to deal with—friendly or off-hand, prompt or slow, efficient or not . . . Note changes in editorial personnel, policy and so on, anything that might be useful in future dealings there (even if it's only 'Never again!').
4. A **'writing only' diary**, or a set of labelled folders, or some other system suited to your particular type of writing. You need to keep track of deadlines, seasonal material, forthcoming competitions and the like.

The cash book

Anything legitimately spent on your writing business—on equipment, stationery, stamps, books and magazines, phone calls, subscriptions, travelling expenses and so on—could be tax-deductible against future earnings, and you might be asked to produce receipts to support your claims.

By law, you must declare your earnings, however modest, in each financial year. The only exception *at present* is that competition prizes are not taxable.

If you spend a lot on postage—and most writers do—it's a good idea to keep a separate postage book, to log details of out-going letters and packages. Enter purchases of stamps, IRCs and postage on packets in your cash book. Log individual letters and other items posted, with their destinations, dates of posting and so on, in your postage book. In this way, you'll have to account (to yourself) for every stamp you use, so you won't be tempted to raid your 'writing' stamps for other letters.

The accepted book-keeping practice is to record debit (money spent) entries on the left-hand page, and credit (money received) entries on the facing right-hand page.

The record book
A loose-leaf book is best for this. You can add pages as you need them. Keep a page for each item you write. You'll be able to see at a glance what's happening to each story, article or poem.

The markets book
Keep a page for each target market, and list every item you send to that market. This is a simple system, easy to keep up to date, and it will help you to avoid misdirected or duplicated submissions.

Before putting pen to paper there are still some important

1992			1992		
June	£	p	June	£	p
2	2 ribbons	5 76	9	Reader's letter	
				(*Woman's Realm*)	5 00
	pkt paper clips	65			
			21	Article: *The Lady*	55 00
	1 ream bond paper	6 50			
	(John Jotter Ltd)				
11	20 x 18p stamps	3 60			
	10 x 24p stamps	2 40			
14	Book: *The Writing*				
	Business	3 95			
	(Bookbuff & Co)				
	Sub renewal:				
	(*Freelance Writing*				
	& Photography)	11 50			
17	Photocopying *Bees*				
	article	50			

Figure 1. Two facing pages from a cash book

matters to consider, which often appear more daunting to budding writers than they need be—copyright, plagiarism and libel.

COPYRIGHT

Copyright simply means 'the right to copy'. No one but you has the right to reproduce, print, publish or sell any part of your writing unless you grant them permission to do so. The law protects your copyright during your lifetime and for 50 years after your death. The copyright is your property, and you can sell it if you wish, outright and for a lump sum, but you would then be giving up all further claim on it, and would have absolutely no right to any money made from that work in the future.

You don't have to register your copyright. It belongs to you the minute you set your words down on paper. (This even applies to personal letters. The *letter* belongs to the recipient, but the *words*

Item: Short story	Title: 'Alien Love'		Length: 1,250 words	
Date sent	Sent to	Accepted/ rejected	Payment received	Date
25.1.92 3.4.92	*Bella* *Woman's Dream*	Rejected Accepted	— £100	17.3.92 16.9.92

Figure 2. Page from a record book

it contains still belong to you, and no one has the right to publish them without your written consent.)

The copyright line you see in books and magazines—the author's name preceded by the sign ©—is a warning to the public that the work is protected. There's no need to put this line on your ms— your work is already protected, and it's highly unlikely that a publisher would steal your material.

However, if you're at all worried about your copyright being

Woman's Dream 11 Milky Way Starville XX7 7XX				Editor: Verity Verucca	
Date sent	Item	Acc'd/ rejected	Pay't recd.	Date	Remarks
3.4.92	Short story: 'Alien Love'	Accepted	£100	16.9.92	Prompt payment on publication. Voucher copy. Nice note from editor asking for more.
17.11.92	Short story: 'The Gemini Factor'	Rejected 5.1.92	—	—	Sudden change of editor. No note with rejection slip. Hold this one till new policy clear.

Figure 3. Page from a markets book

infringed even before you see your work in print, you can
protect yourself quite easily. Just send a copy of your ms to yourself
by registered post, then take the unopened package and your
receipt (make sure the date is clear) to a safe place like a bank.
Deposit it, and get a receipt there as well. You'll then have concrete
proof, if for any reason you have to prove when your ms was
written.

If you're tempted to sell your copyright . . .
You can sell your material outright if you wish, for a fixed one-
off payment. However, you should avoid doing this if you can,
even if the wolf has a foot and a half inside your door. You don't
know what goodies you might be signing away. When the Nazis
occupied Austria, an aristocratic family fled to America. Hungry,
disoriented and unsure of their future, they sold their story for the
price of a few weeks' food and lodging. They signed away their
copyright, and with it all future claims on the story. The family's
name was Von Trapp, and their story became the multi-million-
dollar musical *The Sound of Music*. The Von Trapps didn't get
another cent.

The copyright laws operate both ways
Just as your work is protected from other writers' plundering, so
their work is protected from you. You can't use other people's
writing without their consent, that is, you can't quote any substantial part of another writer's work without written permission.
And that permission can be expensive. At the time of going to
press the recommendations of the **Society of Authors** and the
Publishers' Association for basic minimum fees for quotation
and anthology use are, for example:

● prose: £82-£96 per 1,000 words (world rights)
● poetry: a minimum fee of £30 for the first ten lines plus an
  additional fee of £1.50 per following 20 lines and £1 per line
  thereafter (UK and Commonwealth rights).

Permission to use copyright material should be sought from the
publishers of that material—fees can vary from publisher to
publisher.

Moral rights
The provision of 'moral rights', that is, the rights of 'paternity'

and 'integrity', was introduced in the **1988 Copyright, Designs and Patents Act.**

The **right of paternity** is the author's right to be clearly identified as the creator of a work. The **right of integrity** is the author's right to prevent any distortion or mutilation of the work which would damage his or her reputation.

The 1988 Act requires the author to assert his or her moral rights in writing. (You'll find a notice to this effect in the prelims of many recently published books, especially novels.)

Moral rights are separate from actual copyright in a work. The 1988 Act provides for the **waiving of moral rights,** and some magazine publishers have been trying to insist on writers waiving their moral rights on contributions, some of them to the extent of almost making such a waiver a condition of acceptance. Writers are vigorously resisting this. Should you find yourself faced with this dilemma, do take legal advice.

The Society of Authors publishes a *Quick Guide to Copyright*, and there's a very useful recent book, *Selling Rights* by Lynette Owen. This is primarily 'a publisher's guide to success', but makes informative reading for writers, too.

'Fair dealing'

This term is used to describe the legitimate use of published material 'for purposes of criticism or review'. This is generally interpreted as meaning that you can quote a line or two to illustrate a point you want to make, *provided you give due acknowledgement of the source of the quotation.*

For example, in this book, in the section on writing articles, two short sentences are quoted from Gordon Wells's book *The Craft of Writing Articles* to reinforce a point made in that section. Both the author's name and the name of the book are stated there. This is 'fair dealing'. On the other hand, the paragraph quoted from Liz Taylor's book *The Writing Business*, at the beginning of this book, is printed with the author's *written* permission. It would have been discourteous, to say the least, to reproduce Liz Taylor's words in such a prominent way without her permission, and she would have had good cause for complaint.

We shouldn't forget the gaffe made by Princess Michael of Kent when she wrote her book *Crowned in a Far Country*, and used large chunks of other authors' works without any acknowledgement at all.

It would be safer, then, till you're more familiar with the not too well defined legal niceties, either to avoid quoting from other authors altogether, or to seek permission for anything you want to use. Your request for permission should normally be sent to the publishers, not directly to the author.

Co-authorship

The rule protecting copyright for 50 years after an author's death also applies to writing partnerships, such as an artist collaborating with an author to produce an illustrated book, a lyric-writer and a composer pooling their talents to write a song, or two authors writing a book together. The work concerned doesn't come out of copyright and into the public domain—that is, free for use by anyone—until a full 50 years from the end of the calendar year in which the last surviving partner died.

So don't assume that because one half of a writing team has been dead for the statutory 50 years his work is automatically free of copyright protection. There was an expensive example of this trap in the 1960s, involving the famous partnership of Gilbert and Sullivan, who wrote the Savoy Operas. Pye Records made a jazz album, 'The Coolest Mikado', based on Sir Arthur Sullivan's music for *The Mikado*. Pye released the record in 1961, but were obliged to withdraw it almost immediately at a huge financial loss. (If you come across one of the copies that were sold before the ban, it's a collector's item.)

Sullivan had died in 1900, so his 50-years-after-death were long up. But W.S. Gilbert didn't die till 1911. The jazz arrangements were written and the recording made before Gilbert's copyright ran out, and his copyright protected Sullivan's music. Pye had infringed the joint copyright.

PLAGIARISM

Plagiarism is the use without permission, for your own purposes, of work in which the copyright is held by someone else. There's no copyright in plots, ideas or titles, but you could have problems if, for instance, you follow someone else's storyline so closely that there's a recognisable connection.

In 1987, the estate of Margaret Mitchell brought a complaint of plagiarism against the French author Régine Desforges, in America. Mme Desforges's novel trilogy, published in English as *The Blue Bicycle* trilogy, is pretty clearly recognisable as a re-telling of *Gone with the Wind* in a World War Two setting. The plot and the principal characters have more than a passing resemblance to those of the famous Civil War novel. Mme Desforges has never denied that the American novel provided the inspiration for her books, but she was sued nevertheless, lost her case, and was heavily fined.

You could have problems, too, if you called your book *Catch 22* or *The Eagle has Landed*. Although there's no copyright on titles, this could be claimed to be a deliberate attempt to mislead.

LIBEL

Libel is a statement made in print or in writing, or broadcast on radio or television, which defames the character of an identifiable living person by holding them up to hatred, contempt or ridicule.

Don't be caught out by an unintentional libel. If you make recognisable use, for instance, of a public figure (or even your next-door neighbour) as the model for a character who commits a criminal act, you could be inviting a libel suit.

The same caution applies to the use of names. If you called one of your characters David Owen, made him a GP who had once been in politics, then had him commit a criminal or indecent act, the good doctor would have a pretty strong case against you.

The Society of Authors' *Quick Guides* series of leaflets includes guides to copyright and libel. They cost £1 each, direct from the Society.

2
Preparing and Submitting Your Work

WHERE WILL YOU SEND YOUR MANUSCRIPT?

You should have a clear idea of your target market *before* you begin to write an article or a story. Too many new writers— and some who should know better—write the piece, revise it, polish it up and prepare the ms, *then* start looking for a suitable outlet.

Successful writers seldom work that way. They write with a specific market in mind, a market they've already studied in detail. They tailor the content, treatment, style and length of the work to suit that market.

Market study is just common sense

There's no great mystique about it. Think of your writing as a product you're making for sale. No, don't frown and say you couldn't possibly think of creative writing in that way. If you want to sell your work, you *must* think like that. You're entering a business transaction, little different from selling birdseed or a three-piece suite. You are the manufacturer, and you have to supply what the retailer wants. An editor is a retailer. He buys from the manufacturer—the writer—what he knows he can sell to his customers—his readers.

The fiction editor of *Woman's Realm* won't buy a horror story. She knows she would lose readers. Mills & Boon won't buy a science fiction novel. It's not what their customers expect from them. A literary magazine would have no slot for a DIY article. Yet misdirected mss like that boost Post Office profits year after year.

At the very least, make sure that your ms is targeted at the right area of publishing, an area that publishes *that kind* of material.

SELECTING A MARKET

Start by studying the *Writers' & Artists' Yearbook* and *The Writer's Handbook*. Read right through the section you're interested in—magazines, newspapers, book publishers, radio and television outlets, theatrical producers, wherever your particular interest lies. Don't just look up the names you know. There might be potential markets you haven't even heard of before.

Select those that seem most appropriate, and take a serious, analytical look at them to see what prospects they hold for you, as a new freelance writer. This will give you a useful starting point.

These two writers' manuals, however, don't list all the possible markets. Later in the book you'll find specific sources of information about markets in the various fields. For the moment, let's look at the general principles of market study.

Shoot with a rifle—not with a shotgun

1. Make sure, *before you send anything*, that the market you have in mind is willing to consider unsolicited submissions.
2. Make sure that the content, treatment and style of your work is suitable for your target market.

'Well, I've found a market, but where did I put my story?'

3. Make sure that the length of the piece complies with the publisher's stated word limits.

Let's look at these points in detail, because if you get any of them wrong you won't only lose a possible sale, you could damage your credibility. Careless marketing warns an editor that you're not taking your business seriously.

1. Are unsolicited mss welcome?

Start with the publication itself. Look at the small print at the front or near the end. Many magazines print statements like 'No responsibility taken for unsolicited mss' indicating that such mss will at least be read, or 'No unsolicited mss' meaning that they won't. The *Writers' & Artists' Yearbook* and *The Writer's Handbook* give a good general guide to whether or not you'll be wasting your time sending unsolicited material. Some of the writers' magazines carry regular features on current editorial 'wants', and *Freelance Market News* carries news of current and upcoming markets (you should check the latter news at source, as sometimes it's so new it isn't always complete).

The only 100 per cent reliable source of information is the publisher's own editorial department. If you have any doubts about their willingness to at least read your unsolicited ms, ask them.

If you prefer to write, send a *brief* letter to the editorial department, addressed to the editor by name if possible. If you can't find a name, stick to 'Dear sir' (or 'Dear madam' if it's a feminist publisher):

Dear Melissa Margin,
Do you consider unsolicited material? If you do, would you please send me any available guidelines for writers, or advise me of any subject areas not open to freelances. I enclose a stamped addressed envelope. Thank you.
Yours sincerely

Don't forget the SAE. And be patient. Publishing offices get a lot of mail, and nowadays more than ever are chronically under-staffed. Don't ask for free sample copies 'to study your requirements'. If it's a trade or professional publication, or one you can't find in the shops, ask if they'll send you a copy or two and invoice you for them. If they do invoice you, pay up. Your market study is your responsibility, not the publisher's. It's neither reasonable nor professional to ask another business to subsidise yours.

You can get a quicker answer to your questions, of course, if you ring up the editorial office. Most publishers don't mind this, so long as you don't engage them in a long conversation about your work, or generally take up a lot of time. Just ask to speak to someone in the editorial office if it's a magazine, or ask for the appropriate department if you're ringing a publishing house.

It's a good idea to prepare a short list of questions before you phone, so that you get *all* the answers you need without wasting time trying to remember them off the cuff. The kind of questions you'll probably want to ask are, for example:

1. Do you welcome unsolicited material from freelance writers?
2. Are there any subjects that are written by your staff only?
3. What lengths do you prefer?
4. Do you prefer an enquiry first, or would you rather see the whole ms?
5. Do you have any guidelines I could send for?

Note down, too, any other questions you might want to ask about a particular market. For example, if they answer 'Yes' to Question 1, and you already have a firm idea of what you would like to offer, ask for the name of the appropriate editor, so that you can address your ms or your enquiry to him or her by name. (This helps to get your correspondence on to someone's desk right away rather than languishing in an unidentified pile.)

Don't go into any detail about what you're writing unless they ask you. Be as brief and businesslike as you can. All you need at this stage is basic information.

2. Is your material suitable?

The first and most essential point to establish here is that your subject matter is acceptable and appropriate. As a beginner, you might feel most secure in this if you stick to familiar ground. That is, if you write for publications you already know and like, at least till you have some experience. That old writers' adage 'write about what you know' could be a valuable guide to you here.

You know why *you* buy your favourite magazines, you're familiar with their tone and outlook, so you won't be likely to send them something you wouldn't want to find there yourself. You'd be pretty surprised, wouldn't you, to find a feature on building a drystone wall in *Punch* or a piece on watercolour painting in *Practical Photography*? You wouldn't be likely, then, to send such features to these publications. Yet, believe it or not, people do that kind of thing all the time.

You should be sure that at the very least you choose a market that's compatible with what you want to write.

Getting the tone and language right

The next step is to get hold of a few *recent* copies of your target publisher's products. (It can be worse than useless to use even last year's issues, because editorial policies change frequently.) Make out a study sheet, and analyse the publication, noting down all the points that strike you. Ask yourself:

1. What kind of people are likely to read this publication?
   Age range?
   Sex?
   Types of occupation?
   Their interests and hobbies?
   Their aims and ambitions?
2. Why would they want to read this particular publication?
   For pleasure and relaxation?
   For instruction?
3. Can you detect a clear editorial policy or attitude? Is the publication delivering any kind of message to its readers?
4. What kind of topics and subjects are used in the publication?
5. Are there any topics *not* covered that you might have expected to see there?
6. What areas *appear* to be written by staff members?

The last point is one which might be deceptive to even the most experienced writer. You'll often come across market information and advice that uses terms like 'appears to be staff-written', or 'this looks as if there could be an opening for the freelance'. You should treat this kind of advice very cautiously. Things are not always what they seem. One editor remarked, in response to an enquiry from a writer's magazine about his requirements, that a series he was running was indeed staff-written, but *only because* no freelance had ever offered him anything on that subject, and he was keen to cover it. This is one area where you can only trust 'horse's-mouth' information. Ask the editorial office.

You'll get a lot of help with your answers to these questions if you study the advertisements in the publication. They can give you strong clues about the interests, concerns and age range of the readers.

Look at the language
Now add a section to your analysis sheet in which you look at the language that's used. The kind of questions to ask are:

1. Are the words short and simple?
2. Or more sophisticated and multi-syllable?
3. Are the sentences short and simply structured, with few subordinate clauses?
4. Or are they fairly complex in structure?
5. Is the general tone formal or casual?
6. Are the words, for the most part, formal or colloquial?

The advertisements can help with this too, because they give you a picture in your mind of the kind of people you'll be writing for.

If you pitch the tone and language either too high or too low, you'll have less chance of producing a totally suitable piece of writing. Gordon Wells has a very detailed section on market analysis in his book *The Craft of Writing Articles*. Do read it.

3. Have you got the length right?
Most of the publications and book publishers listed in the *Writers' & Artists' Yearbook* specify the minimum and/or maximum number of words they want for each submission. There's no point in ignoring these word limits. Editors have a certain amount of space to fill, and they won't alter either their policy or the size of their product to accommodate, say, a 3,000 word story if their stated limit is 2,000 words. And they can't tape the excess wordage on to the back cover.

You'll see how to calculate your wordage in the section on preparing your mss.

Keep up to date
You're going into a business that's never static. Magazines vanish, new ones appear. Big publishers eat up small ones. Rebels set up on their own. Editors move about, and often take their pet policies with them, so that their 'new' magazine might quickly become indistinguishable from their last one.

Don't rely on reference books that are even a year or two out of date. You could waste far more money on misdirected mss than it would cost you to replace your out-of-date information sources. Before you send anything off, then, be sure that:

- what you're sending is suitable to the best of your judgement for the publication or publishing house you're sending it to;
- you've written the piece in an appropriate style;
- your ms complies with the publication's stated word limits;
- the publication is willing to consider it;
- your market research is bang up to date.

SHOULD YOU TRY AN AGENT?

Raise the topic of agents at any writers' gathering and you can expect heated argument all round. The most common comment heard from unpublished or little-published writers is that 'agents don't want to know you till you've already made it'.

This might be true as far as some agents are concerned, but it's far more likely that these disappointed writers have had their work rejected by an agent for the same reason most mss are rejected by publishers. They just aren't good enough to publish. An agent won't take on the job of trying to place a book that he or she has no confidence in, any more than a publisher will accept a book he knows he can't sell.

A good agent chooses his clients very carefully, because he'll be committing himself to a lot of work on their behalf. This is understandable when you realise that the agent won't make any money until you do, and what he eventually makes will be a percentage of what your book earns. Contrary to what some writers believe, most agents work hard for their percentages.

If you *can* place your work with a good agent, you'll establish a mutually profitable working partnership. The agent will secure better terms from most publishers, and will have enough knowledge of the markets, both at home and overseas, to see that the rights in your book are exploited as fully as possible. Yes, the agent gets ten per cent of the profits—but *you* get 90 per cent, and that could mean 90 per cent of sales you wouldn't have got without the agent's know-how.

Do try to place your work with an agent if you want to, but be realistic about it. Your chances of a favourable response are about the same as your chances of acceptance by a publisher. Neither will want a substandard piece of work.

There are lists of agents in the *Writers' & Artists' Yearbook* and *The Writer's Handbook*. Choose one who handles the kind of work you've written, otherwise you'll have no chance at all. Most of the agents listed state how they prefer to be approached—by letter, or by sending a synopsis, or by sending the full ms.

Dorothy Lumley runs the **Dorian Literary Agency**. She handles full-length fiction, specialising in women's writing, science fiction, fantasy and horror, crime and thrillers. Dorothy also takes full-length adult non-fiction. She doesn't handle poetry or children's material. Commission: UK ten per cent, US 15 per cent, translations 20-25 per cent, performance rights ten per cent. There is no reading fee. Dorothy prefers first contact by letter, with sample material. Return postage is essential.

> When contacting an agent please give as much information as possible, i.e. whether you already have one and wish to change, a CV of your published works to date, and what you want to write in future. An editor only wants to let an ms speak for itself, an agent wants to know how you view your writing career. If you received any comments on a current ms from an editor who has rejected it, it's useful to pass these on to any agent you approach.
>
> Dorothy Lumley

The partnership of Jane Gregory and Dr Lisanne Radice runs **Gregory and Radice Authors' Agents**, handling full-length mss, fiction and non-fiction. The agency specialises in crime fiction, thrillers and politics. Commission: UK 15 per cent, US and translations 20 per cent. No short stories, plays, film scripts, science fiction, poetry, academic or children's books. There's no reading fee, and editorial advice is given. Approach by preliminary letter and synopsis, with return postage.

Diane Burston handles full-length fiction and non-fiction, *but no longer handles short stories*. Commission: UK ten per cent, US 15 per cent, elsewhere 20 per cent. Approach with a preliminary enquiry, with SAE. Diane now offers a manuscript reading service on a fee-paying basis, on request.

There are lists of agents in both the *Writers' & Artists' Yearbook* and *The Writer's Handbook*, with details of what they handle and what they don't. The Society of Authors publishes a *Quick Guide to Authors' Agents*.

OVERSEAS MARKETS

The whole English-speaking world is open to you. Some of the overseas markets are listed in the *Writers' & Artists' Yearbook*, and *Freelance Market News* carries a quarterly supplement, *Selling Abroad*, which lists current overseas outlets and their requirements.

The USA

The biggest and most lucrative market is the United States of America. The potential for sales there is enormous. For the American markets, however, the marketing strategy is more clearly defined than in the UK. It's universal practice to send a query letter or proposal first, not a complete ms. 'Over the transom' (unsolicited) submissions are vigorously discouraged. Many publishers don't even open the packages—they simply mark them 'Return to sender'.

Writers' guidelines

Before you send anything, even a query letter, your first move should be to write to your chosen targets and ask for their **writers' guidelines**. US magazines issue these as standard practice. It's essential to enclose International Reply Coupons with your request.

These guidelines are very useful. They describe the publication's requirements in detail, telling you what the editors want and how they want you to send it. The guidelines are designed to save time and expense for both the magazine and its would-be contributors.

Writer's Market

You'll find the US markets (about 4,000 of them) listed in the annual *Writer's Market*, a hardback book, well over 1,000 pages long, which also includes many articles and tips on freelance writing. The market information is very comprehensive and detailed, and you're left in no doubt about whether the markets suit your material, and vice versa.

Writer's Market is published by Writer's Digest Books. You can buy it by mail order in the UK from **Freelance Press Services**, or order it through bookshops from Harrap Publishing Group. The 1991 edition costs £12.95 from Harrap. Freelance Press Services will send you a catalogue with their mail order prices on request. They can also arrange subscriptions to the two main

American writers' magazines, *Writer's Digest* and *The Writer*. It can be cheaper, though, to buy these direct from the US, as the magazines often offer special rates for new subscribers. Write for information, enclosing an IRC.

Tips on writing for the US market

1. Always send for guidelines first.
2. At the same time, ask for a copy of the magazine, and enclose enough IRCs to pay for it and for the return postage. Many of the magazines listed in *Writer's Market* specify how many IRCs you should send.
3. Study the sample magazine carefully for style.
4. Invest in an American-English dictionary—many spellings and meanings are different, and it's essential that you write your material in 'American' English.

WRITING SEASONAL AND ANNIVERSARY MATERIAL

Seasonal material

Seasonal material is the term used to describe a book, story, article, poem, song or greeting card whose subject matter relates to a particular season of the year: Christmas, Easter, Hallowe'en and so on.

Seasonal material has to be sent well in advance, anything from three months to a year or even more. It's no use waiting till October to submit a Christmas story to a magazine—the Christmas issue will be ready to print by then.

If you don't already have this information from your target publication, you must check their seasonal deadlines. The quickest and easiest way (all round) is to phone the editorial department and ask. No one will mind, provided you're brief and businesslike.

Insider tip 1
Write your seasonal pieces *during* the season. It can be hard to get into a 'mistletoe and holly' mood when you're drooping over a hot sticky keyboard on a sweltering summer's day. File the piece away, and make a note to remind you when to send it off. Get it out a few days early, and give it an objective, critical reading. You might see faults you didn't notice when you wrote it, and you'll have time now to put them right and to give the work that final polish that can make the difference between a sale and a rejection.

Insider tip 2
Avoid including any reference to current events, unless your piece is intended to be relevant to that year only. Topical references will make it unsaleable in future years.

Anniversary material

Anniversary material is anything on the theme of a past event, written for publication on or near an anniversary of that event. Like seasonal material, anniversary pieces must be submitted well in advance of the relevant date, especially if the event being commemorated is well known and widely documented. As a beginner, you would probably be wasting your time writing about D-Day or a Royal birthday, for instance, unless you've unearthed something new and/or sensational. You could try sending a query letter, but you're likely to find that your target magazine already has something on the subject either in stock or commissioned from a regular contributor or from a famous 'name'.

The *Writers' & Artists' Yearbook* prints a useful Journalists' Calendar of up-coming anniversaries.

Your local papers and magazines might like features about the anniversaries of interesting local people and events, especially if you can link them to something that's happening today. Working from local knowledge, you can start researching early enough to offer the editor a feature packed with facts and human interest— and that's the kind that sells.

HOW TO PREPARE YOUR MANUSCRIPT

There's a standard layout that you should always follow when you're typing short stories, articles or books. (Poetry, playscript and picture-script layouts are shown in the relevant chapters later.) A well presented ms could increase your chances of acceptance. A slovenly one could destroy them.

First impressions count

Your ms says a lot about *you*. Give an editor a crisp, clean, well set out ms, with accurate spelling, grammar and punctuation, and you give him reason to have at least some confidence in its content, even before he reads it. You've shown him you care about what you're doing, and that you're approaching the job in a professional way. Even if he doesn't want this piece, you'll have banked some goodwill for the future.

A sloppy ms won't get a warm welcome. Don't imagine that the editor will toil manfully through a scruffy script, ignoring coffee stains, over-typings, blisters of Tipp-ex, your bald ribbon or your ink-starved dot-matrix printer, in a tireless quest for literary genius. He won't. He might not bother to read much of it at all, because he'll judge, probably accurately, that you won't handle *any* of your business efficiently.

You're offering your work for sale in a highly competitive market. Don't turn your customers off with tatty packaging.

Don't rush it. When you've done a complete draft:

● Check your spelling, grammar, punctuation and syntax.

● Alter any clumsy phrasing or repetitions.

● Check that all personal and place names are accurate and consistent. Page one's brown-eyed Babs mustn't have blue eyes on page five, so check that your descriptions are consistent, too.

● Check *any* facts you're not absolutely sure about. If an editor spots the smallest inaccuracy of fact, he'll start to worry that there might be a big one somewhere.

● Insider tip: When you've read each page for its sense, read it again line by line *from the bottom up*, covering the lines below as you go. This is a proofreader's trick that throws up mis-spellings you can easily miss in a straight reading.

● Finally, check the word count—see below. As you've seen when you read about market study, you should be working with a particular market in mind, certainly by this stage. Make sure *now* whether you need to cut any excess wordage.

Calculating your wordage

Counting every word does *not* give an accurate assessment of the number of printed pages your ms will need. Look at the text of a book or magazine. You'll see that while most of the lines occupy the full width of the text, many do not. Take, for example, lines like:

She looked up.
'Oh no,' she sighed.
'It's true.'

Here you have just nine words—and they use up three lines.

You can see, then, what a distorted picture you'll get if you just count words. You should treat *every* line, however short, as a full line, including the last lines of paragraphs. Think of the whole text area as being solid with words.

This is how to do it:

1. Count the exact number of words in 50 full-length lines. Divide that number by 50. This gives the average number of words per line.
2. Add up the total number of lines in your ms—if it's a novel, take the average number of lines per page over ten full pages, and multiply by the total number of pages in the ms—count short pages at the beginning and end of chapters as full pages.
3. Now multiply the average number of words per line by the total number of pages.

Here's an example:

Total number of words in 50 full lines	=	710
Average number of words per line = 710/50	=	14.2
Total number of pages in the ms	=	193
Average number of lines per page	=	28
Total number of lines in the ms = 193 x 28	=	5,404
Total number of words = 5,404 x 14.2	=	76,736.8

Round this figure *up* to the nearest thousand, so your final word count, the one you would type on your ms, would be 'About 77,000 words'.

With articles and short stories for magazines, it's best to count the actual words, as these are usually set in narrow columns, with much less white space. Round the count up to the nearest ten words.

Make it beautiful
Use good quality, plain **white A4 bond paper** for your top copy. It will have to stand up to a lot of handling and editorial marking if your ms is accepted. Keep a carbon copy, but don't send a carbon to the editor. A good photocopy is usually acceptable.

Make sure your typewriter ribbon is good enough to produce a clear, sharp, black, **easy-to-read type**. Use only a black ribbon, and avoid fancy typefaces (gothic, italic, script and so on). A plain face is much easier to read. If you're printing out from a word-processor or computer, check that the print-out is clear and crisp, and trim the sheets—don't send uncut, continuous print-outs.

Leave **good margins** all round, at least an inch, with a bit more on the left, where space will be needed for typesetting instructions. Keep your pages uniform in layout. Type in **double spacing**. That means leaving one full line of blank space between the lines of type. It *doesn't mean* hitting the space bar twice between words. Type on one side of the paper only.

Even if your machine has the facility to do so, **don't justify** (make even) the right-hand margin. This complicates length calculations. Don't leave extra space between paragraphs, either, but do indent the first line of each paragraph so that there's no confusion about where they begin and end.

Don't underline anything unless you intend it to appear in italics.

Identify your work

Put your name and address on your cover sheet and on the first and last pages of text. Number the pages consecutively, even for a full-length work—don't begin again with 'Page one' at the start of each chapter.

At the top right of each page, type your name, the title (or an abbreviation of it) and the page number. This is called a **strapline,** and it ensures that your pages don't get out of order (or mislaid).

At the bottom right of every page except the very last, type **'mf'**, which means 'more follows', telling the editor and the typesetter that there's more copy to come. Underneath the last line of the last page type 'ends'.

Follow the layout as shown in the example on page 51.

Good reasons for following conventional layouts

It really *is* essential to stick to the conventional forms of manuscript layout. These haven't come about by chance, or been chosen haphazardly. They're the layouts that publishers and printers have found to be the clearest, quickest, safest and least expensive to work on:

● **Clearest** because the double-spaced lines of plain black type on white paper are easy to read and least tiring to the copy editors' and typesetters' eyes.

● **Quickest** because the good margins and double-spaced text

Short story   Patricia Brennan,
                                     21 Our Street,
                                     Printville,
About 1,000 words   Papershire,
                                     England PS99 OXX.

                                     Tel. (001) 101 101

                        The Christmas Kitten

                                by

                           Patricia Brennan

FBSR

Figure 4. Example of a cover sheet

1,000 words

Patricia Brennan,
21 Our Street,
Printville,
Papershire,
England PS99 OXX.

Tel. (001) 101 101

The Christmas Kitten

by Patricia Brennan

It was nearly Christmas. There was snow on the ground and it felt

very cold.

A little black kitten was out all on his own. 'Miaow,' he

said. 'My paws are cold and my ears are cold and all of me is cold.

Oh, I do wish I had not got lost.' But there was no-one to hear the

little black kitten.

He ran along a path and felt a bit warmer then. Suddenly he

saw some light from a house in front of him.

'Perhaps the people there would like a kitten to live with

them,' he thought, so he went towards the light. When he reached

the house, he saw that the light was coming from a back door which

was open. The little black kitten ran inside the house. It was

warm in there and he felt so pleased that he had found this lovely

house.

Suddenly there was a loud bark and a large dog charged into the

kitchen. 'What are you doing here?' he said. 'Don't you know this

is my house? You can't share my food. Go away with you.'

'But I am so cold and hungry,' said the kitten. 'Can I not

stay with you? I won't eat much and I do need a home.'

'No, you can't,' said the dog. 'This is my home and I am not

having any other animals here with me. Be off with you.'

The little black kitten went out again into the cold, dark

mf

Figure 5. How to lay out a page

leave enough room for editorial corrections and typesetting instructions to be marked clearly and rapidly, and also because they speed length calculations.

- **Safest** because their clarity, even after corrections have been marked, reduces the risk of typesetting errors or misunderstandings.
- **Least expensive** because all the foregoing points contribute to speed and accuracy, cutting the time-schedules and reducing the need for costly corrections at proof stage—and so keeping costs down and quality high.

Your observation of the preferred layouts will contribute substantially to your professional credibility.

The cover sheet
The cover sheet for the story shown in the example on page 50 would look something like that shown. The exact layout can be varied, but the important thing is to put all the information there.

FBSR
The abbreviation FBSR stands for First British Serial Rights, and means that you're offering the right to publish your article or story for the first time in the UK. You can only offer this right if the piece hasn't been published in the UK before—if it has, you should give the editor its publishing history in your covering letter.
    The term FBSR is not used for full-length book mss.

The final check
Before you pack up your work for posting, give it a final read through. Make any necessary corrections as neatly and clearly as you can, using a black pen. You shouldn't be making any major corrections at this stage, just tidying up minor typing errors.

ILLUSTRATIONS

Some magazines, especially the heavily illustrated kind, won't consider articles without illustrations. You should find out what kind of illustrations are preferred before you send anything. Black and white prints should be glossy—they give a sharper reproduction than matt-finish ones. Colour pictures are usually submitted as transparencies, which should be protected by plastic covers (never glass). Pack prints between sheets of stiff card.

If your work requires diagrams, maps, line drawings and so on, it should be enough to send roughs in the first instance, or photocopies of the artwork, if you'll be able to supply that yourself. Don't stick your illustrations on to the ms. Pencil *very lightly* an identification number on the back of each one, and pencil the numbers in the ms margins where you want them to go. The page layouts might not allow them to be placed exactly where you indicate, but they'll be placed as near as possible. Type captions on a separate sheet and number them to correspond with the illustration numbers.

PEN-NAMES

You can use a pen-name if you want to. This should be shown in the byline, but *not* above your address. For instance, if Patricia Brennan had wanted *The Christmas Kitten* to appear under the name of, say, Alice Brent, she would have typed her own name and address as shown, but under the title of the story, on both the cover sheet and the first page of text, she would have typed 'by Alice Brent'.

HOW TO APPROACH AN EDITOR

Before we look at the best (and worst) ways of making your first approach, you can be reassured about one thing: no editor will turn down a good piece of work solely because you didn't get your method of contact exactly right first time.

Provided you communicate in a courteous, businesslike way, the editor will either consider your submitted ms anyway, or return it and advise you about the preferred approach.

Find out what to do

It does smooth the way all round, though, if you find out and follow each editor's preferences. You can do this by:

- looking up the publication or publishing house in the *Writers' & Artists' Yearbook* or *The Writer's Handbook*, where the entry should at least give you a clue;
- or phoning a brief enquiry to the editorial office, asking:
  1. 'Do you prefer to see a letter, a synopsis, or the complete script in the first instance?'
  2. 'What is the name of the editor to whom I should address my submission?'

You might be offered some other useful information at this point, too—for instance, that the editor in question is on holiday for a month, or that there's already a large backlog of unsolicited mss waiting to be looked at.

If you can't get hold of any specific information to work from—maybe a phone call over a long distance in peak hours would be too expensive for you—then, in general, it's best to:

- approach a book publisher by letter, enclosing a synopsis
- send the complete ms of a short story
- send the complete ms of an article of less than 1,500 words

---

```
                              Mervyn Fullohope
                              5 Colophon Cottages
                              Upper Case
                              Brighton
                              Tel. (1234) 65789

21st April 1992

Melissa Margin
Fiction Editor
Rosy Dreams Magazine
Queen's Folly Buildings
London E1 1OH

Dear Melissa Margin,

Will you please consider the enclosed short story for
publication in 'Rosy Dreams' at your usual rates.

The story, 'And the Stars were Shining', is about 3,200
words long.

I enclose the customary stamped addressed envelope.

Yours sincerely


Mervyn Fullohope
```

Figure 6. How to write a covering letter

6 Nether Avenue
Satchelmouth
Lincoln

Macdonald Mentor
Editor in Chief
The Southeastern Articulator
London

Dear Mac

I'm enclosing a batch—ten or so—of my short stories. I hope you'll like at least a few well enough to publish them—and pay.

My friends think my stories are a lot better than most of the stuff that's getting published. What do you think? By the way, I've tried one or two other mags, but the editors were stocked up, they said. None of the stories have been published before, so you can have first choice.

I know I'm supposed to enclose a stamped addressed envelope, but you don't have to send these copies back— just let me know what you decide, one way or the other. I'd be *very* grateful, too, if you could give me a few comments about the stories. Any advice at all would be welcome. *Please* don't give me the usual 'The editor regrets' brush-off. It's so discouraging. Sometimes I think editors just don't give a damn about a writer's feelings. I'm sure you're not like that, Mac. A few tips on where else I could try would be useful, too, just in case you don't use short stories at all (I haven't actually seen your magazine—or is it a newspaper?—but I've seen it mentioned a few times somewhere).

Anyway, thanks for your time, and all the best!

Barney Blunder, hopeful writer.

Figure 7. How not to write a covering letter

- send a letter of enquiry about an article of more than 1,500 words.

(See also Chapter 5 for letters of enquiry about articles, and Chapter 6 for details of how to market non-fiction books.)

One professional to another
Every detail of your first approach should be designed to give the editor a positive impression of your professionalism. Here's how to do that:

1. Do enclose a **covering letter**. You want to establish contact with the editor, without appearing either pushy or distant. Your covering letter acts as an introductory handshake. Covering letters and letters of enquiry should be typed as normal business letters, single spaced, not double spaced like mss.

2. Do keep your letter **brief and to the point**. It shouldn't be necessary to tell the editor what your enclosed ms is all about, or to explain the point of your short story—that should be evident from the ms itself or from your synopsis. (A letter of enquiry sent by itself, of course, needs more detail.)

3. Do find out the **name of the appropriate editor** if you possibly can. Many magazines list the various editorial functions, or you can ring the switchboard and ask for the name you need. Failing all else, then 'Dear Editor' is acceptable— just. It's certainly better than 'To whom it may concern' or anything like that.

4. Do enclose an **SAE** big enough and bearing adequate postage for the return of the work. This is a convention that writers ignore at the risk of never hearing of their ms again. Every publishing office has at least one drawer full of unsolicited mss sent without either a return envelope or postage. The editor didn't invite them, so why do these writers expect him to stand the cost of returning them? Small magazines in particular just can't afford to pay for stationery and stamps to return unsolicited material.

And how not to do it
1. Don't send a covering letter that will take the editor as long to

read as your ms would, telling him the history of your life and your writing career and assuring him that your family, friends and writers' group consider you a genius.

2. Don't embarrass the editor with emotional blackmail. His heart will sink and his hackles will rise as he reads that you're unemployed and need the money to feed your children, that you're 99 and unlikely to survive beyond his next issue, or that your doctor has prescribed creative writing as therapy following your nervous breakdown and of course any suggestion of a rejection might tip you over the edge again.

3. Don't be either grovelling, condescending or demanding—just be businesslike. Any other approach will raise doubts about your professionalism, and by implication about whether you'll be reliable and reasonable to work with in the future.

4. Don't send any piece to more than one market at a time—editors won't look kindly on a writer with a reputation for doing this.

5. Don't use umpteen-times recycled envelopes. We all like to save trees, not to mention money, but keep the economy labels and impenetrable layers of Sellotape for your private letters. Economies like this in business correspondence are counter-productive. They project entirely the wrong image, that of the amateur 'scribbler'. And don't send an SAE so decrepit that the editor will cringe and wonder how often it's been licked before. William Brohaugh, editor of *Writer's Digest* magazine, says in his book *Professional Etiquette for Writers* that using recycled envelopes to present your ms is like 'wearing a rumpled suit to a job interview'.

6. Don't, either, use your company's letterheaded paper, or send your ms in envelopes bearing their logo and franked at their expense. This practice has the taint of petty stinginess, and does not inspire confidence.

CHECKLIST

Check these before you make your first contact with an editor:

1. You're contacting an appropriate outlet.
2. You've ascertained as far as you can that you're following the publisher's preferred method of approach.
3. You've checked on the name of the appropriate editor.
4. Your covering letter/letter of enquiry is businesslike and totally to the point.
5. You have not brought in any irrelevancies.
6. You've enclosed a suitable SAE with your story or article, or return postage with your full-length ms.
7. Your stationery is crisp and clean, as is appropriate to your professionalism.

Insider tip

Phrase your letter very carefully, and try to assess the effect your words will have on the editor who reads it. For instance, the following sentences are guaranteed to trigger editorial alarms:

- 'Here is a short story that is a good deal better than those you've been publishing lately . . . '
- 'I am 16 years old, and have decided to make writing my career . . .'
- 'A rejection won't discourage me. It's my life's ambition to get my work published in your magazine, so I'll keep trying till I succeed . . .'
- 'You will appreciate that I am a beginner, which is why I'm sending my work to you before I try to get published in something more literary . . .'
- 'Caution: This story is copyright, and I have taken the precaution of lodging a dated copy with my solicitor . . .'

FOLLOWING UP YOUR SUBMISSION

If you don't get any response within a reasonable time, say two months, contact the company and enquire about your ms, either by letter or telephone. If your follow-up letter gets no response either, you'll have to decide whether you want to try placing your work elsewhere or whether you're so keen on that market that you're prepared to give them more time. It's a sad fact of modern publishing life that most magazines and publishing houses have cut back their staff to the extent that there's usually a large backlog of work.

However, courtesy should work both ways, so if you feel you're being unfairly dealt with, write to the editor advising him that your submitted work is no longer on offer, and that you are sending it elsewhere. Keep a copy of the letter, in case of possible disputes.

HOW TO COPE WITH REJECTION

Rejection—a dismal word for a depressing event: an editor has refused your brain-child. But don't equate rejection with dejection. It happens to (almost) every writer. Hardly surprising, with hundreds of mss jostling for every opening.

The best coping strategy is to build up a regular output. Always have work in hand as well as out 'on spec'. Don't invest all your dreams in one ms. If you're writing novels, start the next one as soon as, or even before, you've sent off your ms to a publisher.

And if your ms does thud back on to your doormat, *please* don't:

● tear it up and throw it away
● iron it and send it straight out again
● write an indignant letter to the editor, questioning his decision, his brains and his origins
● spread jam on his rejection slip and post it back.

What to do

Instead, take some constructive action. Try to analyse what went wrong. Get some practice in developing your most precious asset as a writer—the ability to make an objective criticism of your own work. Ask yourself the questions in the following checklist—and be honest, for, if you refuse to face the truth, you're only fooling yourself.

If you've answered 'Not sure' or 'No' to any of these questions, then you've been less than totally professional in your approach. It doesn't pay to skimp the hard work.

CHECKLIST

	Yes	Not sure	No
1. Are you sure that the work is as good *in every way* as you could possibly make it?			
2. Did you check the accuracy of every fact and reference?			

3. Are you sure you sent the work to   Yes   Not sure   No
   an appropriate market?

4. Did you check *for yourself* that
   your target market is currently
   willing to look at unsolicited mss?

5. Did you check *for yourself* that the
   slot you aimed at is not usually or
   exclusively written by staff or by
   commissioned writers?

6. Did you study your market
   thoroughly?

7. Did you tailor the work to suit the
   style, tone, language and length of
   your market?

8. Did you check your spelling,
   grammar, punctuation and syntax?

9. Did you indicate the number of
   words?

10. Did you present an ms that is
    clean, clear, neat, typed on plain
    A4 white paper, double-spaced, on
    one side of the paper only, with
    decent margins?

What if your answers are all 'Yes'?
Then possibly your ms has been rejected for one of the following
reasons:

● However wonderful you, your best friend, or your writers'
  group believe it is, your work is not up to publishable
  standards. That means that you probably haven't researched,
  organised or written it well enough—or maybe it's just plain
  dull. Sorry to be brutal, but about 90 per cent of unsolicited
  mss fail for these reasons.

- The publisher already has a stock of this kind of material. Yours would have to be sensational to be bought at this time. You're out of luck with your timing—a hazard of freelancing.

- The editor has recently bought/commissioned/published something very similar. He might tell you this. The first two are simple misfortunes. The third would indicate that your market research hasn't been as good as you thought.

- There's been a change of editor and/or editorial policy. That's pure bad luck—*unless* you haven't checked the market recently.

- The editor didn't like what you sent him. If he doesn't bother to tell you this, you'll never know. Another editor might love it.

Two questions
New writers often ask:

'Do editors really read every ms they receive?'
The answer to that is 'Yes'. And 'No'. Yes, they do look at every ms that comes in—no one would consciously risk missing a gem, so everything is looked at. But no, they don't read every ms right through to the end. They don't need to. An experienced editor or publisher's reader can tell from a rapid scan whether a submission is of potential value *to him*. If he doesn't think it is, he won't waste time reading it right through.

It's pointless to get up to the tricks some writers try, to catch out a 'lazy' or 'prejudiced' editor. So forget about the hair or the spot of glue between the pages. They prove nothing.

'Why don't editors tell me where I'm going wrong? Rejection slips are no help at all, so why don't they give me the advice I ask for?'
It's true that very few editors offer advice to writers. Writers, especially inexperienced ones, tend to think this is unfair. However, there are good reasons:

- Lack of time is one. Depending on its scope, an editorial office might receive upwards of 20 or so mss every day. To spend even a few minutes giving constructive advice on every one would occupy much of an editor's working day—and it isn't his job.

- As explained above, an editor doesn't need to read the whole script to know if it interests him or not. He certainly doesn't need to give the ms a thorough critical appraisal. And to try to give a critique based on anything less than a complete critical reading might do more harm than good. You wouldn't be getting a fair criticism at all, only whatever the editor thought might be useful comments based on a very quick scan.

- An editor's job is to find material that's suitable for his publication, not to give writing tutorials. The writing is *your* job. If you send something that is *almost* right, the editor will, more than likely, give you a few pointers and might ask you to do a rewrite for him 'on spec'. But when you submit an unsolicited ms, you have to remember that you're offering goods for sale in a commercial market-place. If you were selling lampshades, you wouldn't ask your customers to show you how to make them, would you?

How books are dealt with

Most book publishers employ freelance readers to assess and report on unsolicited mss. These readers are usually experts in their

'. . . and that's for the story . . . and that's for the poem . . . and that's
for the novel . . .'

field—experienced editors, authors and academics—and it's on their recommendation that an ms is either rejected outright or passed on to a second reader or an in-house editorial team.

A publisher's reader has no authority to accept a book, but his decision to reject one is seldom questioned. The acceptance rate for unsolicited book mss is very low. One publisher's reader says he's only seen two out of the 5,000 or so books he's assessed actually get into print. (This is not the glamorous job many people think it is.)

Do keep a sense of proportion, then, if the first publisher on your list rejects your first novel. You're certainly not alone.

If you must let off steam . . .
Write a nasty letter to the rejecting editor if you wish—but DON'T POST IT. Such a response will not be forgotten, and could prejudice your future chances.

The following 'rejections of rejections' are not recommended either:

- 'Please read this again. I feel sure you must have missed the whole point of the story.'
- 'It was with considerable amazement that I received my returned manuscript this morning. I would have thought that the least you could do was to tell me what you thought was wrong with it. Here is another story. Kindly let me have a swift response to this one, with full details of your reasons, should you reject this one as well . . .'
- 'How could you! Your rejection has cut me to the quick. I may never have the confidence to write another word . . .'
- 'You just don't have the guts to give an original talent a chance . . .'
- 'I am returning your rejection slip herewith. I regret that it is not suited to my requirements at present . . .'

Persistence pays, though
The thriller writer John Creasey earned 774 rejections before he made his first sale.

3
Self-Financed Publishing

IS IT FOR YOU?

It happens occasionally that a publisher lets a potential best- seller slip through his net (*The Day of the Jackal* is often cited as an example). However, publishers don't get it wrong as often as frustrated writers would like to believe. Many, many books are rejected because they're not remotely up to publishable standards. Many others are turned down simply because there is no ready market slot for them.

As a general rule, a publisher accepts a book and finances its publication because *in his judgement* it will add to his profits or his prestige—preferably both. If your offering is rejected by publisher after publisher, but you still feel confident of its merit (or perhaps you relish the adventure of going it alone) there's nothing to stop you publishing it at your own expense—and your own risk. Provided, that is, that you understand just what you're taking on.

Do take a very careful look at what's involved. If you get carried away on a cloud of 'publication at any price' euphoria, you could be in for problems.

CHECKLIST

Is self publishing a real option for you? Before you commit yourself, ask yourself these questions:

1. Do you have the necessary capital to fund   Yes   No
   the venture? It will cost upwards of £2,000
   or so to typeset, print and bind a few
   hundred copies of a very modest book.
   Don't offset any projected sales against
   this—there might not be any.

2. Can you afford to lose this money if it   Yes   No
all goes wrong? Be realistic, because any such
venture has an inbuilt risk factor.

3. Do you know how to prepare the copy
yourself (or are you willing to learn) so that
you can give the typesetter good enough copy
to work from? If not, you'll have to add
these services—editing, typing, checking for
errors, correcting the proofs—to your costs.

4. Have you identified potential sales outlets? (Don't include family and friends who
swear to buy a copy—they'll probably expect
a freebie.) Is there *really* a market for what
you want to sell?

5. Do you have the time, energy and
stamina to go out and sell your product? Or
can you afford the services of a freelance
representative if you want to sell through
bookshops?

If you've answered 'No' to *any* of these, perhaps you should
think again.

WHAT A REPUTABLE PUBLISHER DOES FOR YOU

When a reputable commercial publisher accepts a book for publication, he will:

● enter into a legal contract with you, agreeing the terms under
  which he'll publish your book, and giving full details of all
  rights and royalties agreed;
● possibly (but not invariably) pay you a lump sum in advance
  against the royalties you'll eventually earn from the book;
● arrange all the editing, designing, printing and binding;
● arrange all the advertising, promotion, sales and distribution;
● handle all the accounting work;
● bear the cost of all the above.

He'll do all these things to the best of his ability—because *his* money and *his* reputation are at stake.

You can see, then, how important it is to know what you're taking on. You won't have all this experience, expertise, organisation and finance behind you. You'll be on your own, and you'll be taking all the risks.

Still interested? Then let's get the biggest risk of all out of the way, so that at least you have a fair chance of getting what you pay for.

BEWARE THE 'VANITY' PUBLISHER

He isn't hard to recognise. 'Authors! Does your book deserve to be published? Write to us . . .' he sings from the small ads in the national press. 'Publisher seeks manuscripts . . .'. 'Let us publish your poetry . . .'

What a tempting siren song it is, especially if you're smarting from yet another rejection. But . . .

Reputable publishers do not advertise for manuscripts

Why should they? They're knee-deep already. They can pick and choose. And they choose very carefully indeed, because, as you've just seen, they're risking their money and reputation on their choice.

The vanity publisher risks nothing. He gets his money up front *from you*, and he has no reputation in the business anyway.

He'll give you *no* editorial assessment, advice or service. He'll print your work exactly as you supply it, warts and all. He'll contract to bind only a small proportion of the copies you pay for, with an arrangement to print more as orders come in.

What orders? However many review copies he sends out, you won't get any reviews. Vanity publishers' names are well known in the book trade. No reputable reviewer or publication will feature their products. With the possible exception of your small local bookshop, no bookseller will stock them.

So where does that leave you? Heavily out of pocket, disillusioned and disappointed. Probably angry. And left to do the selling yourself. There's always a risk, too, that you might not even have a book to sell.

One author's bitter experience.
Writer Charles R. Wickins, who lives in the Channel Islands, sent

a short novel he'd written to a publisher called New Horizon, whose advertisements he'd read. He didn't try to place the book anywhere else. It was accepted at once. Mr Wickins's contract promised him 400 copies for about £1,600, to be paid in three instalments. Delighted to be given the chance to 'back his own horse', he sent the first instalment. Then the second. And he waited . . . and waited . . .

He was still waiting, many months later, when an anonymous 'friend' sent him a cutting from *Private Eye* which told him he'd been duped. Shortly after the *Private Eye* exposé, New Horizon's directors 'went abroad'. Mr Wickins never saw a single copy of his book, and never recovered a penny.

Be cautious about poetry, too
Alan Bond is an active campaigner for high standards in poetry. A well established writer and poet, and a popular performer at festivals, Alan has become increasingly perturbed about the activities of some publishers who advertise for poetry to publish. He decided to put one of them to the test.

Before a witness, he dashed off two 'poems' in 28 seconds, and sent them off under a pseudonym. Back came an offer to publish both poems—'Just the kind of contemporary poems we're looking

'A poem called A Host of Golden Daffodils, Mrs Keatsworth? Wonderful! Just the kind of modern, original work we want to publish. Just send your cheque . . .'

for'—in an anthology, if Alan would pay the publisher £7.50 for the publication of each poem. In return, he would get two copies of the anthology, one for each £7.50 paid. If he wanted more, he could have the privilege of buying copies at £4.50 each.

Here are the spoof poems, printed with Alan Bond's permission:

Flying Eyes	By Telecom
And then the bird	He rang.
The big black	I won't be long.
Bird	I waited.
Flew towards my eyes.	He rang again.
I waved my arms	The buses, the taxis, the
The bird flapped a wing	Excuses.
I let it go.	The door waits open.
	I wait and wait and wait.

You can draw your own conclusions about the standard of selection applied by that 'publisher'. Would you be proud to see *your* work published alongside rubbish like that?

Don't risk your reputation

If you want to build up a reputation as a poet, steer well clear of paying to get your work published in an anthology of this kind. No matter how good *your* poems might be, you'll have no control over the selection of the other poems. Your reputation could be badly tarnished, perhaps irretrievably.

Don't fall for these seductive advertisements. The risks are far too great.

YOUR SELF-PUBLISHING OPTIONS

Inexpensive methods

1. You could do the whole thing yourself, with a **typewriter** and access to a **photocopier** or **duplicating machine**.
2. You could produce it on a **word processor** or **computer**.
3. You could have the text set and printed by your **local 'instant print' shop**, and collate the pages yourself. Or there might be a **community press** in your area, with simple printing equipment. Enquire at the library.

Read Jenny Vaughan's comprehensive manual *Getting into Print*, a practical guide covering techniques, design, production, sales and distribution.

Poetry booklets

Joan B. Howes has had many poems published in magazines. She also publishes her own poetry in **booklets** which she sells as fund-raisers, mainly for Animal Rescue. Her booklet *Orange and Sauce* has ten poems attractively printed on card. It cost Joan £75 for 100 copies, which she sold at a small profit through local bookshops. A review in her local paper helped to sell it. Besides raising a little money for a good cause, Joan finds the booklets make very acceptable small gifts, and provide a 'shop window' for her poetry.

PUBLISHING YOUR OWN BOOK

There are several good books available to guide you with an ambitious venture like this. Going it alone can be well worth the effort. Harry Mulholland has certainly found this, with his successful series of mountain guidebooks.

> Self-publishing opens up exciting prospects of promoting projects in which you believe, with complete control of their design and content. Also production time is counted in months, not a year or more. To the usual 10 per cent royalty you add the publisher's profit and the postman can become your friend bringing orders or cheques—not rejected manuscripts.
>
> Harry Mulholland

Harry has put his own know-how and experience into his highly regarded book *Guide to Self-Publishing—The A-Z of Getting Yourself into Print*. The book is self-published (of course), and you can get it through bookshops or direct from Harry's own publishing company Mulholland-Wirral at £7.70 including post and packing.

Recommended books

- *Guide to Self-Publishing—The A-Z of Getting Yourself into Print* by Harry Mulholland—see above.
- *How to Publish Your Poetry*, by Peter Finch. Practical guidance on every aspect of self-publishing from deciding to take the plunge to marketing your product.

- *Copy Prep* by Jill Baker. How to edit and prepare copy for typesetting, how to read proofs and so on. Includes a useful chapter on finding and using freelance services.
- *Editing for Print* by Geoffrey Rogers. A guide to the business and technicalities of publishing, including the various editorial functions, book and magazine production methods, scheduling, budgeting, printing processes and a good deal more.
- *The Craft of Copywriting* and *Do Your Own Advertising*, both by Alastair Crompton. The skills and techniques of promoting and selling just about everything—and an eye-opening read about the advertising industry. These books have a special interest for the aspiring self-publisher. Both originally published by the author as very handsome hardbacks, they were so attractive and successful that Century Hutchinson bought the paperback rights.

Associations
There's an **Association of Little Presses**, which you can join to benefit from its members' advice and experience—see under Associations Open to Unpublished Writers in the Appendices.

Scriptmate
If you're willing (and able) to invest a fairly substantial amount in your project, you can have the whole lot done for you, by **Scriptmate**.

In 1986 Ann Kritzinger launched a high-tech/low-cost printing service to enable authors to publish short-run paperbacks themselves, and to allow publishers to produce short runs of books for market-testing purposes.

Ann was already running her successful editorial advisory service, Scriptmate, and the increasing numbers of good writers being turned down by publishers gave her the idea to extend into the field of high-tech printing. In 1992 she installed the first electronic digital printer in the UK and has programmed it for a quick print production service called **Booksprint**.

The costing system is complex, because every customer's needs are different, and there's a reduced rate for copy supplied on disk, but as a rough guide, a 120 page book, text supplied in manuscript form, would cost somewhere between £1,200, and £1,300 for 500 copies. This is for setting, printing and binding— editorial services are charged separately. There's provision for reordering at short notice, and for converting your book to a much cheaper system suitable for longer runs, should you find yourself with a bestseller on your hands.

Ann has produced a booklet explaining what is involved in self-publishing, from origination to marketing. You'll find details of Ann's *Brief Guide to Self-publishing* under Useful Booklets, page 186.

Full details of all Scriptmate services are available on request.

For writers of academic material

Deanhouse Ltd is a small academic publisher specialising in educational books, academic monographs, occasional papers and academic journals. Deanhouse offers a full editorial and publishing service for individual authors, societies, associations and organisations. The service is also available to overseas authors who want to be published under a UK imprint.

For full details of publishing terms, costs and so on, contact Roland Seymour, Deanhouse Ltd—see Printing/Publishing Services, page 170.

Required by law

You are legally required to send one copy of your publication to **The Legal Deposit Office**, The British Library, Boston Spa, West Yorkshire LS23 7BY, where every publication produced in the UK must be lodged.

Then you'll eventually receive a demand from the **Agent for the Libraries** for a further five copies for distribution to the **copyright libraries** (Oxford, Cambridge, Dublin, Scotland and Wales). You won't get any payment for these six copies, but don't begrudge them too much. Their deposit with the libraries ensures that there is an official record of their existence, which might be useful in the event of any copyright problem. Also, it's to these libraries' lists that libraries throughout the English-speaking world look for potential additions to their lists.

4
Writing Competitions

Cash prizes, publication, prestige, possibly fame—they're all on offer in the hundreds of writing competitions organised every year. Enter as many as you can. You never know what you can do . . .

Paul Heapy read about a science fiction short story competition being run by *The Sunday Times* jointly with publishers Victor Gollancz, who have been building up a strong science fiction list over the last few years. Intrigued by what he read, he decided to enter.

> They did the work for me. Had it been simply an SF story competition, no doubt I would not have entered. After all, I thought of myself as a poet. But J.G. Ballard wrote a superb introductory piece setting out his conception of what SF should be for. And great soul that he is, I could only agree. So when I won, it was just as though they had reached out and tapped me on the shoulder.
>
> Paul Heapy

Paul won first prize, his story was published, and Gollancz invited him to write a science fiction novel. He had never written *any kind* of short story before.

WHAT COULD YOU WIN?

Publication is the most sought-after prize of all. Competitions that guarantee publication of the winning entries attract by far the biggest postbags.

Most prizes are quite modest: a book token or a trophy, or a cash prize that will at least help fund your writing—most cash prizes are between £25 and several hundred pounds.

But you *might* win a spectacular sum like the prizes offered in the Arvon Foundation Biennial Poetry Competition, which amount to many thousands of pounds. There are also large prizes on offer for *unpublished* novels, for instance the Betty Trask Awards for a romantic first novel by a writer under 35, and the Georgette Heyer Historical Novel Prize, both offering guaranteed publication as well as large money prizes.

Have a go at the big ones
Don't be put off entering big competitions by the thought of all the famous writers you might be up against. Entries are often judged on a 'no name on the entry' basis, especially big poetry competitions. The judges don't know who wrote what till the adjudication is complete. There are several ways of organising this, and each competition carries details of its preferred method in its literature and entry forms.

In practice, however, a very big competition is more a gamble than a contest. The usual procedure is that the entries are divided up among a panel of adjudicators, each of whom chooses what he considers to be the best entries from his batch. Then all the judges read all the short-listed manuscripts *only*, so if a judge eliminates your entry in the first round, no one else will see it. From the short-list, each judge selects his potential winners, and from these survivors the eventual winners are chosen—sometimes with a good deal of heat. Philip Larkin once said in public that the poem his three fellow-judges of a major poetry competition had selected as the overall winner didn't make good sense.

WHAT DO THE JUDGES LOOK FOR?

In **short-story competitions**, the same qualities a fiction editor looks for:

- a story that grabs and holds the reader's interest
- a story that stimulates the desire to know 'what happens next'
- a story that is soundly structured
- a story that is fluently written.

Note, *a story*. One of the most common faults judges find is that many writers don't really understand what a short story is and what it is not—see Chapter 8.

In **poetry**, the qualities an adjudicator looks for were summarised by the late Howard Sergeant MBE, who was founding editor of *Outposts Poetry Quarterly* for over 40 years. Howard's criteria are reproduced here by kind permission of his widow, Jean.

They are:

- craftsmanship
- adequate command of the tone and language appropriate to the poem in question
- individual vision and use of imagination
- genuine feeling and personal contact.

In **plays** the criteria used by judges vary enormously because of the differences in the facilities and economics of the companies that organise them. Each competition will give some indication of its requirements in its literature, and it will be an advantage to make yourself familiar with the venue where the winning plays might eventually be performed, so that you can avoid obviously impossible special effects and staging.

ENTERING WRITING COMPETITIONS

The DOs

1. *Do* read the rules. That's obvious, you say? You would be very surprised to see how many people don't bother. Yet it's pretty foolish to risk instant elimination in this way. If you infringe *any* of the rules, you're out—and no one will send back your entry fee.

2. *Do* respect the set word or line limits. The judges *will* notice if you don't, because they are bound by the rules, too. They won't risk the wrath of other competitors by awarding a prize to a piece that's either too long or too short according to the rules.

3. *Do* write what is asked for. Some writers don't seem to realise that, for instance, an article sent to a short-story competition will be thrown out at once. They're wasting their time and their entry fees.

4. *Do* study your 'market'. If the prize includes publication, it makes sense to study at least one or two issues of the magazine or newspaper that will print the winners, so that you can be sure your entry is appropriate. Publication in a national women's or 'family' magazine, for instance, would rule out explicit sex, violence, or over-strong language.

5. *Do* keep a copy of your entry, whether or not the original will be returned (and most competitions don't return entries).

6. *Do* stick to the standard ms layouts, unless the rules say otherwise.

7. *Do* remember that judges, like editors, are human (yes, truly), and could be put off by a badly presented entry.

And the DON'Ts

1. *Don't* be tempted to enter any competition that requires you to give up your copyright. However attractive the prizes, you could be signing away your rights to long-term benefits. Your poem might become a favourite for anthologies or even school text-books, your short story might be adapted for radio or TV—it might even be the basis of a series—and you would have no claim at all to *any* payment.

2. *Don't* wrap your entry up in elaborate packaging. Fancy folders, decorated cover-sheets, ribbon bows and suchlike are just a nuisance to the organisers, and will go straight into the waste bucket. One organiser remarked that she had received a Jiffy-bag containing a cardboard document wallet inside which was a mass of tissue paper covering a plastic sleeve, all to protect a single poem. It's odd, too, how the fanciest packaging, according to adjudicators' reports, almost invariably contains the worst entries.

3. *Don't* forget to enclose your entry fee. Your entry will be disqualified without it, and it's most unlikely that the organisers will send you a reminder.

4. *Don't* be too devastated if you don't win. Remember that all competitions are a lottery to some extent. Just keep trying. It's wonderful practice in writing to set lengths about set subjects —and remember Paul Heapy.

CHECKLIST

Check these points before sending off a competition entry:

1. Have you read *all* the rules?

2. Is your entry appropriate to the competition subject?
3. Is your entry suitable for publication (if applicable)?
4. Is it within the stipulated lengths?
5. Have you typed it in the standard layout?
6. On white A4 paper?
7. Have you kept a copy?
8. Have you understood and followed any special instructions about anonymous entry and so on?
9. Have you enclosed the correct entry fee, and made your cheque or postal order payable to the designated name?
10. Have you enclosed an SAE if one was requested?

WHERE TO FIND OUT MORE

- Writers' circles, literary groups and creative writing classes receive regular information.
- Your local library might have leaflets. Ask at the desk if none are on display—some organisers request that their leaflets should be kept for those interested enough to enquire, rather than left out to be used as shopping-list scrap-paper by browsers.
- Writers' magazines like *Quartos, Freelance Writing and Photography, Writer's Monthly, Writers News, Writers' Own Magazine* and *Freelance Market News* list current and forthcoming competitions.
- The *Friends of Arvon Newsletter* has a competitions column.
- The *Writers' & Artists' Yearbook* and *The Writer's Handbook* list major literary awards.
- The Book Trust Information Service.
- Flyers distributed by most small literary and poetry magazines.
- National newspapers and magazines carry notices of major competitions, and some run their own.

5
Writing for Magazines and Newspapers

WRITING ARTICLES

Take a look at your newsagent's shelves. Did you realise that nearly all the publications you see there buy most of their articles from freelance writers?

The constant demand for good articles makes them one of the easiest types of writing to sell. 'Easier to sell', however, doesn't mean easier to write. The demand is high, certainly, but the standard expected is also high.

Potential outlets

There are literally thousands of potential outlets for articles. The *Writers' & Artists' Yearbook* lists over 600 UK newspapers and magazines that publish (and pay for) articles. *Willing's Press Guide* lists more than 10,000 UK publications, including trade, professional and specialist magazines, and many of these welcome freelance contributions relevant to their subject area.

Freelance Market News and the Bureau of Freelance Photographers' *Market Newsletter* are good sources of information about current markets for articles.

To write and sell freelance articles, you need:

● the ability to write clear, concise English;
● an observant eye;
● an enquiring mind;
● a professional approach to writing up your material.

To succeed at article writing, you must study a market regularly—editors' needs change—and slant your writing to meet that requirement.

start off with a good strong 'hook' and try to end strongly too. For a saleable writing style, keep words, sentences and paragraphs short and simple. And keep on writing.

Gordon Wells

A MANY-SPLENDOURED MEDIUM

Never mind how new you are to writing, there's sure to be at least one facet of article-writing that could give you your first taste of publication. Look at the choice:

- factual articles
- personal experiences
- human interest stories
- opinion pieces
- 'how-to' and DIY articles
- 'round-up' articles (where a number of people contribute ideas/experiences/opinions)
- self-help and self-improvement
- interviews
- profiles
- travel features
- short-short articles and fillers
- and you'll probably add more as you explore the possibilities.

Make it shapely

Whatever your subject, an article needs to be structured into a logical and satisfying form. Like a good story, it needs a beginning, a middle and an end, but unlike a story, where you can take liberties with that order of things, an article works best with the most straightforward sequence:

1. **A strong opening paragraph.** If you've dug up some amazing or little-known fact, or if you have a strong statement to make, put it here. For example, you might open an article on *Writing as a Second Career* with: 'Politician Douglas Hurd spends his spare time writing political thrillers—and he gets them published. How many other famous people have a writing career as a second string?'

    It's quite a common misjudgement for beginners to save their juiciest fact till the end. But if you don't grab the reader's attention right away, he might not bother to read to the end, so your amazing discovery is lost anyway. Feed him the tastiest titbit first, and save the second-best to the last.

2. **The middle**, the main course. This should be packed with interesting information written in the most logical sequence, but not simply given as a list of facts. Spice it with anecdotes, questions, opinions.

3. **The closing paragraph.** This should provide a satisfying rounding-off, summarising in some way what you've been saying. It's a good idea to refer back, however obliquely, to your first paragraph: 'Given the chance, would Douglas Hurd give up politics to write full-time?' Or give your reader a question of his own to consider: 'Would *you* give up your day-job to risk writing as a career?' If you do have another interesting fact to offer, you could conclude with that: 'Agatha Christie's main career was writing. So was her second string. She wrote six romantic-psychological novels under the pen-name of Mary Westmacott. These novels, as she wrote in her *Autobiography*, were the only ones that really satisfied her. Her crime novels were her bread and butter.'

Shorts and short-shorts

The terms 'short articles' and 'short-short articles' sometimes puzzle new writers. These terms don't really have any strict definitions. What would be considered a short article by one magazine might be a full-length feature to another. Generally speaking, however, you can work on the basis that:

- A **short-short article** is 200-500 words.
- A **short article** is 500-750 words.
- An **article** is usually 750-2,000 words.

Always check the length preferences of any particular market, as a matter of course, before you send them any material.

Fillers

A **filler** is a short item fitted into a small space so that a page won't be left with blank spaces where the main items are not long enough to fill it.

Anecdotes, humorous verse, puzzles, jokes, cartoons, tips and hints, press errors, odd facts, brain-teasers, quotations—all these are used as fillers, and many magazines buy them from freelances.

Keep an eye open for likely filler slots, and collect odd pieces of information, jokes, 'overheards' and suchlike that fall your way.

Readers' letters

These, too, come into the category of fillers, but they've acquired a status of their own and are now a strong selling feature for many publications.

Payment can be quite high. *Woman's Realm*, for example, pays £25 for their 'Letter of the Week'. The average payment is £5-10, and some magazines 'pay' in prizes instead of cash.

'Letters to the Editor' are a popular starting point for many new writers. Don't be misled into thinking that because they're short they're easy to write and sell. A successful letter has probably been worked on just as carefully as any article—it has to be tailored to its market, too.

Every publication has its own style. Look at points like:

- Does the publication prefer long or short letters?
- Is the tone of the letters neutral? cosy? argumentative? cynical? amused? helpful? sympathetic? belligerent?
- Do any of the letters raise controversial issues?
- Are any of the letters obvious responses to correspondence or features that appeared in previous issues of the magazine?

Readers' letters are very good practice for an aspiring article-writer because they demand the same kind of disciplines: no waffle, no wordiness, and the letter must make its point as clearly and concisely as possible.

You can use pen-names if you like. Editors might not want to see the same names appearing too often in their letters pages.

No SAE required

'Readers' letters' is one area where the normal convention of enclosing an SAE doesn't apply. Letters are never returned, and are only acknowledged if they're used. Voucher copies are not sent. You might receive advance notice that your letter will be printed, or you might hear nothing at all till you get your payment.

WRITER'S BLOCK

Before we go on to discuss the various types of writing, let's take the mystique out of this much-discussed 'affliction'.

Sometimes called 'frozen brain syndrome', writer's block is very often a self-inflicted problem. You stare at the blank page. You *want* to write. You drink yet another cup of strong coffee. Still nothing comes. Why?

The reasons are seldom mysterious, muse-dependent or beyond your control. Ask yourself the following questions:

Non-fiction

1. Do you **care** about your subject? Does it move you, excite, annoy, thrill, disturb, infuriate, inspire you? Do you really have something to say about it?

2. Or did you choose it because it looked like a potentially **marketable** subject? It didn't look too challenging? Because you were stuck for any other ideas? Because you feel it doesn't much matter *what* you write as long as you write something?

3. Assuming you do have something to say, have you **researched** the subject thoroughly, and formulated your own ideas about it?

Fiction

1. Do you really want to write fiction? Or do you equate 'being a writer' with 'being a fiction-writer'? (Be honest with yourself— you're unlikely to succeed if your heart isn't in it.)

2. Assuming that fiction *is* your field, have you taken time to think about your **characters**—what kind of people they are, what has made them that way, how they're likely to behave, reacting to and interacting with each other in the situations you plan for them?

3. Have you prepared a convincing **background** from knowledge and experience and/or research?

4. Have you experimented till you've found the right **storytelling viewpoint** and character?

5. Have you allowed **time** for your story to simmer, to build in your mind till it's boiling over and you can't wait another minute to get it down on paper?

In other words, are you trying to write either something that's more of a chore than a pleasure, or something that is not yet ready to be written? Most cases of writer's block result from either lack of involvement or lack of preparation. The cure is in your own hands.

WHAT WILL YOU WRITE YOUR ARTICLE ABOUT?

Your best bet if you're a beginner is to write about something you know well. The better you know your subject the more confidently you'll handle it, and your confidence will communicate itself to your reader. And don't forget that the first reader who will see your article is an editor. An experienced editor can sense at once if a writer is trying to tackle a subject he isn't really comfortable with.

Your knowledge of the subject will probably already have given you some knowledge of the publications that might be interested in printing your articles. You'll need that knowledge, because without doubt you'll be able to write more than one article on your subject, each slanted to a different market.

For instance, if your hobby is collecting old gramophone records, you could write about

● where to find them;

● how to store them;

● how much they cost;

● the equipment needed to play them;

● the artists who made them;

. . . and much, much more, as the subject diagram on page 83 shows.

Try making your own subject diagram. Write down the main subject in the middle of a (large) sheet of paper, and write its main branches all round it. You'll quickly see how the branches begin to shoot out sub-branches, and probably even the sub-branches could produce twigs. This kind of lateral thinking is a lot more productive than simply making a linear list. It's a very powerful brainstormer.

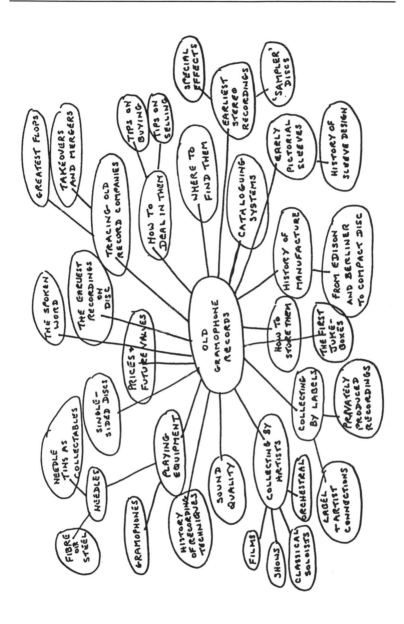

Figure 8. How to make a subject diagram

What do you know already?

You can use the same exercise to draft out your knowledge of sources of information on your subject, and on possible markets. You'll find the ideas coming almost faster than you can write them down.

Make it convincing

Whatever your subject, you should make it your business to gather enough information and solid facts about it to write a convincing, fact-packed article. The editorial nose will quickly sniff out a 'scissors-and-paste' job—that is, a piece cobbled together from reference books and other people's opinions. That doesn't mean, of course, that you can't make use of other people's findings and conclusions (provided you don't infringe their copyright), but your article will be stillborn if it contains little or nothing of your own thoughts and feelings.

You'll often find, too, that it will take several rewrites to achieve a convincingly 'spontaneous' style. Don't be afraid to let your own personality show through.

Be methodical

You'll save yourself a lot of irritation, time and trouble, if you devise a simple system for filing your article and filler information as you gather it. It's infuriating if you're stuck for one small piece of information and you can't remember where you put it.

You need to be able to retrieve the information you need, quickly and easily, the minute you want it. This is especially important if you're trying to fit your writing into precious spare time sandwiched between your day job and keeping the weeds under control.

You can use document wallets, large envelopes, card index systems, or, of course, electronic storage if you have a word processor or computer. The system itself doesn't matter—what *does* matter is that you have one.

But don't let the research take over your writing time too much. As Gordon Wells says in *The Craft of Writing Articles*: 'You need to be able to find facts quickly and easily. But your hobby is writing—make sure that it does not become "fact-filing".'

Where to look for information

- Your local library. If you tell the library staff what you're looking for and why you want it, you'll find them very helpful.

'And that's only the rejection slips.'

- *Research for Writers* by Ann Hoffmann is an indispensable source of information about how and where to find information.
- Newspaper cuttings. There are lists of press cutting agencies in the *Writers' & Artists' Yearbook* and *The Writer's Handbook*. A subscription to such an agency could be an excellent investment, especially if you specialise.
- Specialist book dealers. There might be one locally—look in *Yellow Pages* or ask at the library. There are many listed in the *Book and Magazine Collector*.
- **The British Library Newspaper Library** at Colindale, North London, houses London newspapers from 1801, and English provincial, Scottish, Irish, Commonwealth and foreign newspapers from 1700. You need to apply to the Library for a reader's pass.

HOW TO SELL YOUR ARTICLES

It's becoming more usual now to send a **query letter** before you submit an article. This has long been the accepted practice in the US, and most American editors insist on a preliminary query. Material that comes in 'over the transom' is now discouraged.

In general here in the UK, though, it's still all right to send a short article—up to about, 1,500 words—as a complete ms. It would take an editor nearly as long to read a query letter as it does to scan a short piece. You won't get a firm acceptance on the strength of a query anyway, unless the editor knows your work already, so you might as well let him see what you can do. If he prefers a preliminary query, he'll let you know when he gives you a decision on your submission.

Longer pieces are another matter. It's better to query the editor first, not only to save postage and stationery costs, but also because if he does express an interest, he might have some suggestions to make about your treatment of the subject, perhaps preferring that you take a different approach or that you make it shorter than you suggested and so on.

How to write a query letter
Your query should tell the editor three things:

1. What the subject of the article will be, and what angle you intend to treat it from. Use the 'bullet' system to list your points briefly and clearly. Include an indication of the proposed length.

2. Why you think his readers would be interested in what you have to say.

3. Why *you* are able and qualified to write it. If you have special qualifications—practical experience, a degree in the subject, or something like that—then include them here, but avoid dragging in qualifications, however impressive, that are totally irrelevant to the subject you'll be writing about. If you want to offer an article on, say, collecting Commonwealth commemorative stamps, your target editor is unlikely to rush off an acceptance letter because you've told him you've been practising yoga and transcendental meditation for 20 years.

Suppose you want to offer the editor of a general interest magazine an article on collecting ephemera, those throw-away bits of social history: postcards, programmes, tickets, bookmarks and the like. First, check that you have a note of the current editor's name, correctly spelled. Then structure your query something like the letter on page 87.

```
                                              Emily Hoarder
                                              White Elephants
                                              Overflow Lane
10th January 1989                             Fillingham

David McColl
Editor
Annabel
D C Thomson & Co Ltd
185 Fleet Street
London EC4A 2HS


Dear Mr McColl
```

I am writing to enquire whether you would be interested in seeing an article about collecting ephemera.

There's plenty of scope for building up an interesting and potentially valuable collection, without too great a financial outlay. Many of your readers might be unaware of how collectable these scraps of social history have become. Some readers might not even know that such a field of collecting exists.

To begin a collection they would need to know:

* what the term 'ephemera' means: essentially items of no intrinsic value, such as postcards, cigarette cards, bookmarks, tickets, magazines and newspapers, advertising material, pamphlets and so on;

* where to look for collectable items: antique and collectors' fairs, where a few dealers specialise in ephemera, jumble sales, charity shops, the attics and cellars of friends and relations...;

* approximate prices they might expect to pay;

* where there is most potential for value increases;

* the best ways to store and/or display their collection.

Once a new collector begins to realise how wide the range is, he or she often moves on to specialisation, and is soon hooked on the hobby. It's fun, it's fascinating, and it's relatively cheap.

I have been collecting ephemera myself for several years, and have recently begun to specialise in bookmarks, their design and history, and their value to the companies that issued them (they were widely used as an advertising medium).

I can supply a variety of photographs, if you wish.

The text as I plan it would be 1,750-2,000 words. I enclose a stamped addressed envelope for your reply.

Yours sincerely

(Mrs) Emily Hoarder

Figure 9. How to write a query letter

BOOKS ABOUT WRITING ARTICLES

- Lisa Collier Cool, *How To Sell Every Magazine Article You Write*. An American book on the techniques of selling by query letter before you write the article. Some writers swear by this method, and some editors prefer it, but others say it's a waste of time, preferring to see the finished article. You'll have to find out for yourself if it works for you.

- Anthony Davis, *Magazine Journalism Today*. Following the progression of magazine production from planning to publication, including much useful insight and advice on how material is commissioned, and how it is best written, both by in-house staff and freelances. Very enlightening analyses of what makes good feature articles and interviews. Covers research as well as writing.

- Fay Goldie, *Successful Freelance Journalism*. Practical advice on writing and selling all kinds of articles from fillers to features, and tips on developing a freelance career.

- Brendan Hennessy, *Writing Feature Articles*. A practical guide to writing successful features—how to gather, organise and target information.

- John Hines, *The Way to Write Magazine Articles*. Covers researching, writing and selling. Good on developing ideas.

- Raymond Hull, *How to Write 'How To' Books and Articles*. Good American book showing in detail how to communicate your knowledge to readers. Covers collaborating, research, illustrations and promotion.

- John Morrison, *Freelancing for Magazines: A Guide for Writers and Photographers*. Exactly what it claims to be. Articulate, comprehensive and thorough.

- Kit Sadgrove, *Writing to Sell, The Complete Guide to Copywriting for Business*. Intended primarily for the business and advertising writer, this is an invaluable book for all writers. It's packed with practical advice and examples of how to structure your writing and how to choose and use words to the best possible effect.

- Gordon Wells, *The Craft of Writing Articles* and *The Successful Author's Handbook*. Thoroughly practical, easy to understand and packed with examples and advice on writing and selling. Two of the best books around.

- Gordon Wells, *The Magazine Writer's Handbook*. Lists specific magazine markets, giving editorial requirements, payment rates, how to approach the editor and so on. Useful as a guide, but make sure you only use the latest edition. Even then, check the information, because the magazine scene is so volatile at present that some of the information will be out of date almost before the ink is dry.

- Gordon Wells, *Photography for Article Writers*. A practical guide to taking the kind of photographs that will help you sell more articles. Like all Gordon's books, it's thoroughly sensible and down-to-earth, and an enjoyable read, too.

JOURNALISM

A successful journalist is a writer who knows how to:

- tell his story within tightly focused limitations;
- see his story from his reader's angle;
- avoid verbosity and cut out padding;
- express his meaning in clear, concise and unambiguous language;
- produce quality work under pressure, to meet tight deadlines.

Robbie Gray is former chief sub-editor/night-editor of the *Daily Mirror*, *Daily Express*, *Sunday People* and *The Star*. Asked what advice he would offer to aspiring journalists, Robbie said:

I have only to repeat the advice of Sir Hugh Cudlipp when he was editor of the *Daily Mirror*: 'Keep it simple.'

It was also Cudlipp who said: 'Never talk down to your reader.' It took me some time in my salad days to work out precisely what he meant—and, of course, it was exactly that. Never try to give the readers the impression that you think you are cleverer than they are. Never deliberately try to send them scurrying off in search of a dictionary. They don't have time, and probably won't bother.

Robbie Gray

Most newspapers, like most magazines, buy material from freelance writers. There are three main types of newspaper: national, regional and local. The *Writers' & Artists' Yearbook* lists all the nationals and a few of the regionals, but *The Writer's Handbook* gives a lot more information, listing all the major national and regional titles, with editorial names and requirements, tips about approaching them, and what they pay.

The financial rewards

Payment varies a good deal. Some papers pay NUJ (National Union of Journalists) rates whether you're a union member or not. Others pay 'by arrangement', in which case you'll be offered what the editor thinks the piece is worth, or possibly, if he's never heard of you, what he thinks you'll be prepared to settle for. This is one of the areas where a thoroughly professional approach can really pay off. Don't invite the editor to offer you less than he might have done because your badly presented and carelessly spelled mss and your tatty recycled envelopes leave him in no doubt that he's dealing with someone who doesn't know the business.

Unless you're already a member of the NUJ, there's little use in arguing about the offer. You can either refuse it and try your luck elsewhere or you can accept it philosophically, so that you can add another item to your portfolio of published work. A strong portfolio will eventually put you in a position to negotiate fees.

NUJ rates go up to about £200 per 1,000 words for a feature in a national daily newspaper, and about £235 per 1,000 words for a feature in a national Sunday newspaper. Provincial papers pay a good deal less, but they certainly should pay *something*— you won't be doing either yourself or other writers any favours if you write for nothing.

Getting your foot in the door

Local papers are your best bet to begin with. They always want:

● news stories, short and to the point, to cover local events: 'Her Majesty unveils memorial plaque', 'Local Grandmother's surprise triplets';

- social issue articles: 'Save our swimming baths', 'Do our citizens want clean streets?';
- striking photographs of local people, places and events.

(Note the strong 'local' emphasis.)

The five 'W's
When you're writing your article, make sure you haven't omitted any essential information. Check the content against the journalist's creed, the five 'W's:

- Who?
- What?
- Where?
- When?
- Why?

And if it's appropriate, add an 'H'—How?
   Whether they're distributed free or not, these papers live on

---

Invoice

(999) 34123   Oliver Columnist
                                                12 Gossip Alley
                                                Tiny Tiles
                                                By Eastborough

22nd July 1988

Basil Bond
Editor
Eastborough Tattle
Eastborough

To writing one short feature, 'Scandal
   at the Vicarage', published in
   Eastborough Tattle 15.7.88.   £25.00

Figure 10. Example of an invoice

their advertising revenue, so short pieces stand a better chance of acceptance because they leave more room for ads.

Include a photograph or two with your article if you can. Check with the paper about preferred sizes.

Find out, too, about deadlines—this week's hot news is next week's rejection.

You'll usually be paid after publication, at some set date, and you might be expected to submit an **invoice**. Clarify this beforehand. An invoice is a simple business document, a bill asking for payment of money which is due to you. It's easy to prepare. Just make sure you include all the necessary information, as in the example.

Articles have to be straightforward and to the point—there is little room for picturesque speech. Most important of all, facts should be absolutely accurate. Dates should be given where applicable, since while it may be obvious to you that last Sunday means last Sunday, in the chaos of an editor's office such things cannot be taken for granted. Dated material gets first priority, and in any case, it is professional procedure. If I ever quote anyone then I usually enclose a separate sheet giving details of how they can be contacted, and then the editor can verify or expand an interview, or perhaps arrange a photograph.

Give names and dates in full. There should be no reason for the editor to think you haven't done your job properly.

Writing factual pieces imposes its own discipline on the writer, and this is particularly healthy for those writers who are just starting off.

Graham Thomas

You're never too young to start writing for publication. Graham Thomas started at 15, and was soon selling regularly to his local papers. He's now at university studying English and Philosophy, and hopes to make writing his full-time career.

Is there a gap in the coverage?

If you spot an opening for a topic your paper isn't already covering, you could suggest ideas, perhaps for:

- a book, film, TV or video column;
- a poetry corner;
- a children's page;
- an original series that *you* could supply on a regular basis.

But don't suggest any kind of competition unless you're willing to handle the entries yourself. The staff won't welcome the extra work.

A new book

Freelance Writing for Newspapers is a recently published book written by Jill Dick, who has been a journalist all her working life. From her experience both as a staff journalist (on *The Sun*, the *News of the World* and the *Manchester Evening News*) and as a very successful freelancer, Jill gives the kind of practical advice and information that is invaluable to every writer who wants to write for the press.

JOURNALISM FOR DISABLED PEOPLE

Physical handicap needn't be a barrier to a successful writing career. Anyone who doubts that need only look at the achievements of Christy Nolan, overall winner of the 1987 Whitbread Awards.

> We all go to our Maker taking with us a host of untapped talents and for you this may be writing. You never know whether you can write until you try. Because it is a home-based activity which can be followed at any time of the day, writing is a good occupation for disabled people, particularly wheelchair riders. It widens social horizons and uses much of the time of which handicapped people have plenty. You are not disabled to your readers, and you compete on even terms with able-bodied writers.
>
> Pat Saunders

Pat Saunders averages 60,000 words of published material a year. He is confined to a wheelchair and unable to hold a pen. Currently he is Assistant Editor of *Practical Caring* magazine, a magazine specially geared to the interests and concerns of caring relatives.

When Pat began writing a weekly column for disabled people in the *Portsmouth News*, he was surprised to find that this was the first regular feature of its kind in the country. Convinced of the widespread need for such features, he produced *All Write Now*, a booklet of practical advice and encouragement for disabled people who want to write, particularly those who want to communicate the kind of news and information that would benefit other disabled people. You can order a copy by post—see under Useful Booklets on page 186.

6
Writing a Non-fiction Book

Are you an expert on a subject that would interest a large number of people? Do you have first-hand experience or knowledge that might benefit, profit, intrigue, amuse or inspire others? Have you set up and run a successful business? Built your own house? Prospected for gold in the Andes? Perhaps then you've already thought of writing a book about it, but didn't know where to begin.

IS YOUR IDEA FEASIBLE?

Before you commit yourself to the project and all the hard work it will involve, ask yourself these questions:

1. Is the subject big enough for a book? *An Encyclopedia of Houseplant Care* would be. *How to Water Your Aspidistra* wouldn't.

2. Would the subject interest a wide enough readership to make it a commercial proposition? Books do get written and published on some pretty obscure topics, but they're usually intended for a specialist market. It depends on how wide a readership you want to reach, and on whether it's mainly profit or prestige you want. It also depends on finding the right publisher for your subject. There are many publishers who might want an *A-Z of Microwave Cookery*, but not too many who would consider taking on, for instance, *Advanced Theory of Semiconductors*.

3. Is the subject one that will attract the book-buying public as well as library stockists? The biggest potential sales are in books on self-improvement, health, food and diet, leisure activities and hobbies. Do-it-yourself titles sell well, and books on cookery and gardening waltz off the shelves. 'How-to' books are

in constant demand, especially those that show how to make or save money. An American publisher, asked by a beginning writer if he thought anyone would ever write *the* 'Great American Novel', advised: 'Forget the Great American Novel. What this country needs is a good book on how to repair your own car.'

You've got a suitable subject—so how do you tackle it?
First, break it down into manageable sections. The prospect of getting 30,000 words or more down on paper can be pretty daunting. Split it up into ten or 12 chapters of about 3,000 words each, and it loses much of its terror. It becomes more like writing a series of articles on your topic.

Divide your subject on paper, then, into ten or 12 sub-themes. These will eventually form your chapters. Under each sub-theme heading note all the information you already have that's relevant to that section. Make notes (different coloured inks help) of any obvious gaps in that information. You'll have to do some research to fill those gaps.

Now comes the crunch
Do you have, or do you know how and where to find, enough material to write each of your chapters—at least 2,500 words— *without waffle or padding?* Can you realistically expect to pack every chapter with interesting and relevant information?

If not, abandon it, and look for a more suitable subject. Don't throw away your notes, though. You've probably got enough material there for several articles at least.

If, on the other hand, you're sure there's enough solid material, enough factual information for a book, then go ahead and prepare your proposal.

But don't write the book yet. If you don't find a taker for your idea, you don't want to have wasted your time writing an unsaleable book. If a publisher does express an interest, he might want to make suggestions about the way you write the book—a different kind of treatment, perhaps, from the one you originally envisaged. If you'd already written the whole book, you would then have to do an extensive rewrite.

NOW TO PREPARE A PROPOSAL

First, you need to make an **outline** of the complete book. Set down your title. The publisher might want to change it, but for the purposes of the proposal, you need a **working title**. Make it as snappy as you can. *How to Raise Funds for Charity* is more effective than *Organising Successful Events to Raise Money for Charitable Projects*. It would fit the spine of the book better, too.

Write down the first chapter heading, and set out underneath it, briefly, all the points you intend to deal with in that chapter.

List all your chapters in this way. Then juggle them into a logical sequence. This is the skeleton of your book, the bones on which you'll build the meat.

Type the outline neatly in single spacing, like a letter (this is a document, not a working typescript)—an extract from such an outline is given on page 97. Indicate the proposed overall length of the book. If illustrations would be appropriate, say whether or not you can supply them. The publisher will advise you if he prefers to arrange this himself.

The synopsis and sales pitch
On a separate sheet of paper, type out:

- a short, concise explanation of the book's proposed purpose and area of interest;
- your reasons for believing there's a need for it;
- an indication of the market you envisage for it;
- a few words to show that you know what the competition is like;
- your reasons for believing that your book will be better.

An example of such a synopsis is given on page 98. Be sure to keep copies of these papers.

APPROACHING A PUBLISHER

Look through the publishers listed in the *Writers' & Artists' Yearbook*, and draw up a list of those who specify that they handle books of the kind you plan.

Before you act on this list, ask at your library if they can access a **Writers' Database** on computer or if they have a copy of Whitaker's *British Books in Print*, to find out which of your proposed target publishers have recently published a book on your subject. It's best to leave those publishers off your primary target list. Unless you could offer something radically different in your

Part of an outline for a proposed book: How to Raise
Funds for Charity

Introduction:
A short general overview of the choices for raising funds
as an individual, a small group, or a larger group run by
a committee. It will also draw attention to the need to
know how the law affects various activities - this will
be covered in one of the chapters.

Chapter 1: How to set up a committee
This will show the various offices - chairperson,
secretary, treasurer and so on - and will define each
office and the responsibilities it usually carries,
stressing the importance of allocating the right job
to the right person. For instance, it's hopeless to
appoint as Treasurer someone who can't tell an invoice
from a receipt.

Chapter 2: Fund raising and the law
What you need to know about how much you can do without
permission, what you need permission for - for instance,
you can't sell raffle tickets door-to-door without a
special permit - and what you can't do at all.

Chapter 3: How to draw up a provisional programme of
events
Your committee needs to decide what is within its
members' capabilities and what isn't. For instance,
there's no point in trying to organise a jumble sale if
none of your members is willing to sort out the jumble.
It's no good, either, deciding to have a brass band
concert if the nearest brass band is based a hundred
miles away and you would have to meet its travelling
expenses.

This chapter will include a list of suggestions for
events: a summer fair, a Christmas craft fair, an
antiques and collectables fair, a car boot sale, a raffle,
an auction, a dinner dance and dozens more.

It will also point out the areas where you need
special insurance and safety precautions.

Figure 11. Outline for a proposed book

Synopsis: <u>How to Raise Funds for Charity</u>

The book will cover all aspects of fund raising, from individual efforts (making and selling crafts, holding a coffee morning, hosting a sales party and so on) to large committee-run, business-sponsored events like dinner dances and concerts.

It will be spiced with accounts of various real-life achievements - I know of a man who raised many thousands of pounds for a hospital by hiring Concorde and flying a party to the USA - which will intrigue, encourage and inspire the reader.

Legal, health and safety aspects will all be covered. There will be suggestions for a comprehensive range of money-making possibilities, and a directory of contact addresses: services, suppliers, information sources and so on.

I believe that there are many people who would be attracted by having so much information offered in one handy volume. It would be useful both to individuals and to organisations: clubs and societies, schools and colleges, hospital support groups, church groups and many more.

As far as I have been able to ascertain, there are very few publications on sale on the open market that gather together so many facts and suggestions and combine them with an interesting and entertaining narrative.

And one of the essential ingredients for success in any enterprise is surely that the participants should enjoy the venture from the outset. The necessary literature should also be part of the enjoyment.

Figure 12. Typical synopsis for a proposed book

approach to the subject, your proposal would start off at a disadvantage there.

Decide which publisher you'll approach first. If you possibly can, find out the name of the editor responsible for the type of non-fiction book you're going to offer. Ring up the company's switchboard and ask the operator. If the operator doesn't know, ask him or her to put you through to the editorial department for non-fiction books. Just ask whoever you speak to there for the appropriate name, and make sure you know how to spell it. Don't try to discuss the book on the phone unless you are specifically asked to do so—all you want at this stage is the right name, so that you can be sure your proposal will reach the right person as quickly as possible. *The Writer's Handbook* includes many editors' names as contacts in the various houses listed there, but it's as well to check up, as publishing personnel move about a lot.

Your covering letter
This should be brief and to the point. All the information about your proposed book is in your proposal, so there's no need to repeat any of it in the letter.

If you have any special qualifications for writing the book, you should mention these—but only mention *relevant* matters. Your degree in metaphysics won't persuade an editor to accept your book about fund-raising—it has no relevance. Your experience in the field does, though. All you need is something on the lines of:

> Dear Mr Corn-Harvester
> I enclose a synopsis and outline of a book I am preparing about fund-raising for charity. I've had 15 years of experience in this field, both in active organisation and in administration. Would you be interested in seeing the manuscript?
> Yours sincerely

Send the letter with the outline and synopsis, and remember to enclose an SAE.

Prepare a sample chapter or two
You might have to wait a while for a reply, or you might have to try several publishers before you get a nibble of interest. Spend this waiting time working on a couple of sample chapters (not necessarily the first ones) and on gathering the information you're

going to need to fill the gaps you noted when you were making your original notes.

When a publisher does express interest, he'll probably ask you to send him at least one chapter, so that he can see whether or not the content will live up to the promise of the proposal. He'll also want to assess your capabilities as a writer before he commits himself any further, so you must make your sample as good as you possibly can.

When you're offered an agreement

If your sample is satisfactory, the publisher will either ask to see the completed ms 'on spec' (in which case you should think very carefully before committing yourself to finishing the book with no definite prospect of acceptance) or he will offer you an agreement on the strength of what he's already seen. With the agreement, he *might* also offer you an advance against royalties.

The *offer* of a book contract entitles you to apply for membership of The Society of Authors and/or The Writers' Guild of Great Britain. Either of these organisations will advise you about the agreement you've been offered, so as soon as you receive the document, contact them and they'll scrutinise it on your behalf, *before you sign it.*

You should read up on the subject of contracts, too. The Society of Authors' *Quick Guide No. 8: Publishing Contracts* is concise and helpful, and Michael Legat's book *An Author's Guide to Publishing* has a lot of information on the topic.

BOOKS TO HELP YOU

- Anthony Blond, *The Book Book*—gives an insider's view of the publishing world. You'll see just what's involved in selecting saleable mss.

- Giles N. Clark, *Inside Book Publishing*—aimed at those seeking a career in publishing. This will give you a knowledge of what people who work in publishing houses actually do in the production of books from blockbusters to academic texts, including the finding and developing of publishable books.

- Raymond Hull, *How to Write 'How-To' Books and Articles*—gives practical advice and lots of detailed instruction.

- Michael Legat, *An Author's Guide to Publishing* and *Writing for Pleasure and Profit*—both good on this topic, and useful on contracts, too.

- Ian Linton, *Writing for a Living*—includes non-fiction books, and covers proposals.

- Dan Poynter and Mindy Bingham, *Is There a Book Inside You?*—how to make a book, even if you can't write it yourself. Plenty of advice and know-how.

- Gordon Wells, *The Book Writer's Handbook*, *The Successful Author's Handbook*, and *Writers' Questions Answered*—practical and down-to earth advice, and common-sense strategies for getting non-fiction published.

- Neil Wenborn, *How To Get Published*—outlines the whole process of getting non-fiction books published; an ideal introduction to the subject, and excellent value for money.

SOME PUBLISHERS WITH STRONG NON-FICTION LISTS

- **Argus Books Ltd:** modelling, woodwork, crafts, field sports, new technology, all hobbies and leisure topics.

- **B.T. Batsford Ltd:** chess, lacecraft, hobbies, animal care, fashion and costume, photography, sport, games, theatre, transport, travel.

- **Blandford Publishing:** animal care and breeding, art and graphics, humour, gardening, hobbies and crafts, sport, games, magic and the occult.

- **David & Charles:** crafts, gardening, travel, leisure and hobbies. They'll send you their *Authors' Guide* free on receipt of a first class stamp.

- **How To Books Ltd:** 'achievement' paperbacks on careers, employment, expatriate topics, student life, business skills, parenting, community and life-style development. (The publishers of this book.)

- **Merehurst Ltd:** books for the creative, leisure and home reference markets, crafts, cake decorating, cookery, natural history.

- **Mitchell Beazley Ltd:** illustrated non-fiction only—all subjects.

- **Northcote House Publishers Ltd:** business, professional, educational, travel.

- **Pan Books Ltd:** paperback house publishing a comprehensive range of non-fiction subjects.

- **Pelham Books Ltd:** autobiographies of sportsmen and women, sports handbooks, practical handbooks on pets, hobbies, crafts and pastimes.

- **Thorsons:** self-improvement, health, cookery, medical, alternative medical, crafts and hobbies.

7
Specialist Non-fiction

THE RELIGIOUS PRESS

Magazines catering for all religious denominations need inspirational and educational material. Most of the religious publications in the UK are related to the Christian faith in its various denominations—*The Catholic Herald, The Tablet, Christian Herald, Church Times* and many others. You'll find other religious publications listed in the *Writers' & Artists' Yearbook* and *The Writer's Handbook,* including several well-known Jewish publications like the *Jewish Chronicle* and the *Jewish Telegraph.* Many smaller religious groups publish their own papers and magazines.

If your interest lies in this direction, you're probably already familiar with the publications relating to your own faith, but you might not have thought of them as markets for your writing.

Whatever your religious persuasion, however, you should apply the same basic principles for successful writing: study each publication as an individual market, because they're all different and will look for material that satisfies their particular interests and outlook.

There's also a society for writers of specifically Christian material, **The Fellowship of Christian Writers**.

Some publishers of religious and theological books

- **Darton, Longman & Todd** publish Christian books of all types, and welcome unsolicited mss, synopses and ideas for books.

- **Lion Publishing plc** publish a wide range, from board books for the very young to adult reference, all with a Christian viewpoint. They welcome unsolicited mss, synopses and ideas that are suitable for a general and international readership.

- **SCM Press Ltd** publish religion and theology, and some philosophy, and ethics. Unsolicited mss and synopses welcome 'if sent with an SAE'.

- **SPCK** (Society for Promoting Christian Knowledge) publishes general religious titles and pastoral books including popular self-help.

Most cities and large towns have at least one religious bookshop. You can browse in these and look for the publishers whose books reflect your own religious interests. If you can buy one or two, so much the better—you could then enlist the shop staff's help for advice about appropriate publishers. Your library, too, should have information on religious publications.

A book on writing for the religious press
Writer's Digest Books publish a very good book on religious writing, *Writing to Inspire* by William Gentz and Lee Roddy.

EDUCATIONAL WRITING

You don't have to be a teacher to write educational material. Teaching experience helps, certainly, in preparing course material or textbooks, but the most important requirement is skill in communication.

The educational writer has to work within fairly strict guidelines. Content, language and structure must be geared to specific ages and abilities. You can get information on courses and required syllabus material from local education authorities, career centres and libraries. If you are a teacher, you have an advantage here over the 'outsider', because you're in touch with current needs.

There are openings, however, for those with no teaching experience at all. What is needed is the ability to write well to specific guidelines.

English language teaching
The English language is taught all over the world, not only to children but to people of all ages. Most of this teaching is done with storybooks, not textbooks. Some of these are original stories, but many are adapted from modern novels and from the life stories of famous people—Marilyn Monroe, Charlie Chaplin, Winston Churchill . . . Popular, too, are non-fiction subjects like airports,

animals, earthquakes, the sinking of the Titanic, the Olympic Games and so on.

What's required is 'a good read' that keeps the learner turning the pages so that he absorbs the language almost without thinking about it. These abridgements and adaptations have to be prepared within tight disciplines according to varying levels of ability. At the lower level, for example, you might work with

- a given word list of, say, 300 words;
- a given list of simple sentence structures;
- very simple tenses.

With these as your basic 'bricks', you build a story, or, for an adaptation, you use the existing storyline. You would be asked to work within specified wordage limits.

If you think you could make a go of this kind of tightly disciplined writing, contact publishers with an English Language Teaching (ELT) department, citing any relevant qualifications and writing experience, and including any story or adaptation ideas you might have.

The Society of Authors publishes a 16 page set of Guidelines for Educational Writers, which you can buy direct from them.

Reference books
These can be a very good publishing proposition, because they're steady sellers. There are reference books on every imaginable subject, from wildflowers to monastery sewerage systems. If you have an idea for a reference book—perhaps you've spotted a gap in the market—and have enough knowledge of the subject to write it, approach a publisher with a proposal as outlined in Chapter 6.

Some publishers of educational books
- **Cassell**
- **Hodder & Stoughton**
- **Kogan Page**
- **Longman**
- **Macmillan Education**

And of reference books
- **W. & R. Chambers**
- **How To Books Ltd**
- **Kingfisher Books**

- **Macmillan Academic & Professional**
- **Northcote House**
- **Oxford University Press**

There are many others—consult the *Writers' & Artists' Yearbook* and *The Writer's Handbook.*

TRAVEL WRITING

Successful travel writing involves much more than descriptions of journeys and exotic locations, or quoting from brochures and guide books. A travel article or book should:

- provide insight into the people's lives and culture;
- create a sense of atmosphere;
- bring a place to vivid life through details rather than generalities;
- get the facts right, but treat them imaginatively;
- be descriptive without being overloaded with superlatives, clichés and fulsome adjectives.

Too many aspiring travel writers concentrate on descriptions of beautiful sights seen through the windows of their car or tourist coach. You need to spend time absorbing the local atmosphere, talking to the people, taking photographs and making on-the-spot notes of your impressions—not just what you see, but what you feel, what attracts, what repels, what arouses your curiosity. Dig beneath the surface, be sensitive to the implications of what you find.

If you need inspiration, don't turn to guides or brochures—read Jonathan Raban, Eric Newby, Jan Morris, Paul Theroux . . . the best travel writers can transport the armchair traveller into the heart of another place, another culture. They make you *feel* the thin air of the Andes, *see* the grandeur of the Victoria Falls, *smell* the sweat that built the Pyramids, *hear* the echo of the jackboot in the streets of Warsaw.

Travel writing has more in common with fiction than with journalism. It needs much more than facts, figures and descriptions —it needs the pulse of life. If you can achieve this, you'll delight the editors who receive your mss.

Don't forget the photographs. They could be vital in clinching a sale.

A book to help you
- Morag Campbell, *Writing About Travel*

Some publishers of travel books
- **Marion Boyars**
- **Cape**
- **Gollancz**
- **Mitchell Beazley**
- **Pan**

Magazines
Many general interest magazines publish travel articles. You need to be able to offer something specific, in most cases, focusing on an unusual aspect or region. Avoid areas that have already been done to death. Good photographs will help your writing sell.

Overseas magazines could be interested in pieces about the UK, which, of course, is 'abroad' to all other countries.

TECHNICAL WRITING

To be a successful technical writer, you need many of the qualities and skills of an investigative journalist. You need to know how to sift essential information from masses of data, then represent that information in terms that are easily understood by the people who need it.

To be a technical writer, you would need:

- to enjoy researching, possibly into subject matter you know little or nothing about, in enough depth to clarify the subject to people who need to understand it;
- to have enough knowledge of human relationships to win co-operation from the people who hold the information you need—you might have to apply a little psychology when you deal with a temperamental genius (or, even worse, with someone who thinks he's a genius);
- to possess a logical mind and a good memory;
- to be able to present your findings in clear, concise, un-ambiguous English, without resort to specialist jargon.

It's that last point that prompts many businesses to employ writers from outside the company to prepare sales brochures, users' manuals and suchlike. Company employees can be too close to the subject to see that what is commonplace knowledge to them might be a complete mystery to the layman or non-technician. If you've ever torn your hair out over a computer handbook you'll recognise the problem. An 'outsider' sees the gaps and the areas of possible confusion because he needs to get them clear in his own mind before he can pass them on to his readers.

Courses

Tutortex Services of Ulverston offer an Open Learning Correspondence Course in Technical Authorship. Tutortex students are also eligible for the appropriate City and Guilds examinations, and for possible grants and sponsorship. Tutortex will advise you. There is also a self-tuition course in Technical Authorship, supplying all the teaching and self-assessment material but not the tutoring and marking given in the full course.

For further information contact the Enrolment Secretary, Tutortex Services, 55 Lightburn Avenue, Ulverston, Cumbria LA12 0DL. Tel: (0229) 56333.

Literature on the subject

* J.A. Fletcher and D.F. Gowing, *The Business Guide to Effective Writing*
* Ian Stewart, *The Business Writing Workbook*
* Ian Linton, *Writing for a Living*

The Society of Authors publishes a useful pamphlet, *Sell Your Writing*, which costs £1.50 direct from them. Compiled by Andrew Nash and the society's Technical Writers Group, this is mainly intended for business and technical writers, but gives guidelines for all writers who want fair dealing in selling their writing.

COPYWRITING

Copywriting for business can be very lucrative. The main areas are **advertising** and **direct mail**. To get a feel for what's needed, stop skipping the adverts and binning your 'junk' mail. Somebody has been paid to write all that material, and paid very well. Maybe you could do it, too, and develop a useful sideline or even a new career writing copy designed to sell products and services.

You could start by offering your services to local companies. Study their promotional material. Could you write it better? Can you think of a more effective approach? If so, let them see it. Show them what you can do. Present fresh ideas and sharp persuasive language.

As Kit Sadgrove says in his new book *Writing to Sell*, 'The language of advertising is different from the schoolroom.' Whether you're writing press releases, adverts, sales literature, newsletters, posters or TV and radio commercials, you need to know how to construct good copy and how to avoid the pitfalls. This book would be an investment for any writer who wants to sharpen up his or her word and structure skills, and could prove invaluable if you're interested in copywriting as a commercial prospect. It's aimed at businesses wanting to improve their own promotional literature— *your* writing skills could help small businesses in particular to do this better and at less expense than could a large advertising agency.

Recommended books

- Kit Sadgrove, *Writing to Sell—The Complete Guide to Copywriting for Business*
- Alastair Crompton, *The Craft of Copywriting*

8
Short Stories

You shouldn't listen too much to writers who complain that 'You can't sell short stories these days—editors don't want them . . .'

Comments like that are almost invariably made by unsuccessful writers who don't—or won't—recognise the true situation. The popular magazines can't get enough short stories. *Good* short stories. Well written, entertaining, *publishable* short stories.

Editorial desks groan under dull, clichéd, sermonising stories, lifeless, formless, pointless stories, sad, sordid, despairing stories . . . Editors don't want them. Their readers don't want them.

In 1984, when *Woman's Own* decided to stop reading unsolicited fiction (the first British women's magazine to do so), editor Iris Burton told a writers' magazine that reading the hundreds of mss they received every year was highly time-consuming and almost totally non-productive. (Since then, many other magazines have adopted this policy, for the same reason.) Good short fiction was 'as hard to come by as ever', Iris Burton said, but far too few writers really study the market, and to be commercially successful a writer must combine creativity with pragmatism. She had to buy much of their fiction from America, where writers take a much more professional and analytical approach.

There you have it, the key to writing successful, saleable short stories: *a professional and analytical approach.*

TEACH YOURSELF TO WRITE STORIES THAT SELL

A saleable short story needs a structure (beginning, middle, end), a plot, a theme, sound syntax and grammar, and language appropriate to its subject and to its intended market.

You can learn how to do it. There are classes and seminars, courses and books that specialise in short-story writing You can read, study and analyse published short stories by past and contemporary writers.

Let's look at some aspects of fiction-writing that seem to trouble new writers in particular.

How to find plots

Every plot begins with an idea. And ideas are everywhere. They're all around you—and inside you, too. Fantasy novelist Ursula Le Guin, quoted in the American magazine *The Writer* (October 1991) says that when she's asked where she gets her ideas, she replies: 'I don't get them, I am them; a writer's life is her ideas, her work, her words.'

Try this: every day for a week, read your daily and Sunday newspapers from cover to cover (advertisements and all) and clip out *every* item that arouses even the mildest interest. Letters to the editor, the life-style sections, reviews, financial and sports pages as well as news stories—skip nothing. Collect anything that intrigues.

Then browse through them, and let your imagination run free . . . What made that young girl so desperate that she left an apparently happy and comfortable home to live rough on city streets? Why did that householder go to such lengths to prevent his neighbour uprooting a dying section of their commonly-owned hedge? How did that woman fare when she returned to her job after winning her case for unfair dismissal? Would being 'Slimmer of the Year' change a man's life more than it would a woman's? What if . . . and if . . . ?

Beware plot 'formulae'. 'Dial-a-Plot', or 'The Miracle Plot Menu' might seem to offer an easy way to write brilliantly plotted stories, but in fact they're a waste of time and money. Good plots stem from the actions, reactions and interactions of characters, not from any artificial recipes or manipulations of events. You want something that's fresh and uniquely yours, not some stale, clichéd, over-used plot that will make the editor groan 'Oh no, not *that* one again!'

Keep a notebook with you at all times—the germ of a really original plot might bubble up in your brain at the most unexpected moment. Don't lose it.

Viewpoint

This is simply the point of view from which the story is told, that is, through the eyes of the hero or heroine or any other character, either in first person or third person, or by an 'omniscient' storyteller who sees and hears everything.

It's a very useful exercise to take one of your stories and write it several times, from the viewpoints of different characters. Does the story work better from any particular viewpoint? Is it more convincing? More intriguing? More exciting? Can you analyse *why*?

Some stories almost demand to be told from several different viewpoints. This is more likely with novels than with short stories, though, as there is usually less scope for jumping from one character's mind to another's within the limited action and wordage of the short story. If you do decide on the multiple viewpoint, it's best to avoid changing viewpoints within a scene. This can diffuse the impact, and possibly confuse or irritate the reader.

For the beginner, it's probably best to tell your story from the viewpoint of a single lead character. This will help to hold your story together by giving it a stronger emotional focus.

Then you need to decide whether first person or third person narrative would serve your story best. This is often simply a matter of taste and suitability. Try it both ways, to see which works best for your story. If you opt for first person, be careful not to fall into the trap of 'The Big I syndrome', where hardly a line is written without use of 'I', 'me', 'myself' or 'mine'. Too many first-person stories are ruined by this ineptitude, which can make even an exciting story boring and repetitive. Take a highlighter pen, and mark every use of 'I' and so on—you'll soon see if you've over-peppered your story in this way.

HOW TO BE YOUR OWN EDITOR

Don't shy away from revising and rewriting—your words aren't chiselled in stone, and self-criticism is a valuable skill to acquire. It pays to be ruthless at this stage, however painful you find it. These are some of the faults and weaknesses that are likely to affect an editor's decision:

1. Is the **opening** too long? Too slow? Too general? It's vital to grip the reader's interest, curiosity and emotions right away.

2. Have you **begun** in the right place? Begin at an intriguing point in the action. You can feed in information about previous events as the story progresses.

3. Is there too much **flashback**? Too much scene-setting through characters' memories can kill the story's pace.

4. Are your **characters** fully developed, and portrayed through their actions, reactions and interactions rather than by bald exposition?

5. Have you sustained **momentum** through the middle section, moving the story forward through cause and effect, building towards the **climax**? Or have you cluttered the narrative with unnecessary detail and superfluous characters? (Seeing an old woman begging in the street might remind your hero of his good fortune despite his present troubles, but we don't need to know how Betty the Baglady came to fall on hard times.) Keep the focus where it belongs.

6. Is the **ending** satisfying, believable, and logical in the story's own terms? Or did you run out of steam, leave unintentional loose ends, or cheat your reader with a contrived 'twist' or a hitherto unseen character who appears with all the answers?

7. Is the **viewpoint** consistent? The tiniest shift can destroy the reader's empathy. For example, your hero sees his lost love: 'David felt his heart thump, and tears began to sting his blue eyes . . .' The single word 'blue' takes us from inside David's mind and asks us to observe him from outside, making us look *at* him rather than feel *with* him.

8. Have you chosen suitable **names**? Inappropriate names could 'place' characters in age bands or social categories different from those you intended: 'Ada and Herbert', 'Tracey and Kev', 'Lucinda and Peregrine' evoke different perceptions.

9. Is the **dialogue** natural? Or does it seem stilted and unconvincing? Read it aloud, tape it if possible, and listen for awkward phrases and out-of-character speech patterns and vocabulary. Use abbreviations—'couldn't, 'he'd', 'they'll' and so on—where they feel right.

10. Have you allowed the reader to use his **imagination**? Or have you described every move, every thought, every feeling? We don't need to know every detail. Leave some gaps for your

reader to fill in. This will help to give your story pace, too.

11. Is your **spelling** sound? Careless spelling can alter or fog your meaning—and it gives the editor negative messages about you as a writer.

12. And your **punctuation**? Inaccurate punctuation can produce nonsense: 'The water was pouring down Carol' doesn't mean the same as 'The water was pouring down, Carol'.

13. And your **syntax**? Syntax is the ordering of words to convey a clear and unambiguous meaning. Consider this: 'The mayor arrived to light the bonfire with his wife.' All the right words are there, but their order makes the statement absurd. Check that you've actually said what you intended to say.

14. Are your **tenses** consistent? It's very easy to shift from present to past and vice versa without noticing.

15. Is your writing **concise** and **sharp**? Or wordy and slack? The more compact your prose, the stronger its impact. Especially avoid weak verbs that need adverbs to clarify their meaning: a branch *fell heavily* to the ground—try *thudded*.

16. Have you used *active* rather than *passive verbs*? 'Fido chased Felix' is stronger than 'Felix was chased by Fido'.

17. Have you avoided **vagueness**? 'There was quite a crowd waiting to see the parade' is woolly—try something more positive: 'Crowds waited ten-deep along the parade route.'

18. Is your text **repetitive**? Don't bore your reader with 'Mary's mother said this' and 'Mary's mother said that', 'Suddenly this' and 'Suddenly that' . . . Vary your vocabulary.

Be ready to learn

Painful though it may be to a writer's ego, it is a fact of life that editors really do know what is best for their own publications, and occasionally they tell us so. Such comments may be pithy and wounding or sweet and encouraging. Whichever, take note, and never be too clever to learn.

Diann Greenhow

Diann Greenhow worked as a secretary for 20 years, then in 1984, with her children at school, and bored with 'mere house-keeping', she enrolled in a writers' correspondence course. Blessed with a diligent and compatible tutor, she has recouped the cost of the course many times over, with short stories and humorous articles sold to a variety of publications, including several D.C. Thomson magazines and 'true story' magazines. She says her acceptance rate is climbing steadily, but she still writes a lot more than she sells, and regards herself as very much a raw beginner.

If you're still dreaming of your first sale, that might seem strange, but Diann has serious ambitions to be a romantic novelist. Her successes so far, she says, are due to perseverance with her chosen markets. When her stories were rejected, she analysed them and tried to work out where she had gone wrong. Then she tried again. Gradually the rejected stories began to come back with some editorial comment instead of the usual rejection slips. She studied these comments and acted on them. And tried again. And again. Now her hard work is paying off.

WHERE ARE THE MARKETS?

Let's look at just a few, to give you a start. Then you must dig them out for yourself, from your newsagent's shelves (make friends with him first), from writers' magazines, the *Writers' & Artists' Yearbook, The Writer's Handbook, Freelance Market News*. Don't just look at the obvious markets. Search among the specialist publications—some of these, like *Darts World* and *Canal and Riverboat*, will sometimes consider short fiction that's directly relevant to their area of interest. Some regional magazines and newspapers, too, publish short stories.

The popular women's magazines

You don't have to be a woman to write for women's and family magazines. You don't even have to write 'women's' stories. Keep up with the new publications that appear throughout the year. The weekly magazines *Best* and *Bella* each publish one short crime/mystery story and one longer short story in every issue. That means slots for 208 stories every year. *Take A Break* publishes 'twist-in-the-tail' short stories, about 1,000 words. *Me* also publishes short fiction, but prefers a query first—don't send your ms.

Some women's magazines prefer male writers to adopt a female pen-name, but more and more masculine bylines are appearing.

Publishers D.C. Thomson & Co Ltd are very helpful to promising new writers. They're always on the alert for writers who can supply the right kind of fiction for their publications, which include *Annabel*, *My Weekly* and *People's Friend*. As well as short stories, they need serial stories for the weekly magazines, and short romantic or romantic-suspense novels, 35-40,000 words long, for *My Weekly Library*.

> D.C. Thomson are always in the market to find good new writers for their wide range of publications, as shown by the many different leaflets we provide.
>
> New writers have to face the fact that competition for success is fierce. Because of the volume of contributions received, encouragement to new writers from editors can only go to those who show most promise in producing our kind of material.
>
> Once you have studied the market, send your story to the editor of the magazine at which it is aimed or to the Central Fiction Department which acts as a clearing house for unsolicited contributions.
>
> The Fiction Editor, D.C. Thomson & Co Ltd.

Note the phrases: 'our kind of material' and 'once you have studied the market'. You have to show not only better than adequate writing ability, but also an awareness of the company's needs. They offer encouragement and advice, not tuition in writing.

D.C. Thomson will send you their guidelines on request. These leaflets include writing for their women's magazines and for *My Weekly Library*. They also have leaflets available on writing children's and teenage picture- and photo-story scripts, and will send you details of how to submit your mss.

A few more markets, for a variety of short stories

- *Acumen* magazine, editor Patricia Oxley—includes original short stories. Patricia looks for well written stories that avoid worn-out ideas and clichéd phrases.
- *Stand* magazine, editors Jon Silkin and Lorna Tracy—publishes original fiction, including experimental and sometimes controversial work.
- *Interzone*, editors David Pringle and Simon Ounsley—publishes only science fiction and fantasy/horror stories.
- *Alfred Hitchcock's Mystery Magazine*—an American magazine publishing well-plotted, plausible mystery, suspense, detection

and crime stories up to 14,000 words. Send a self-addressed envelope and an IRC for guidelines.

● *Ellery Queen's Mystery Magazine*—another American magazine, publishing high-quality detective, crime and mystery stories, 4,000-6,000 words. 'We like a mix of classic detection and suspenseful stories.' 'First Stories' slot, by unpublished writers.

You should *always* study at least one issue of a magazine before you send any work to it, to familiarise yourself with its style and flavour. Not every magazine, of course, will suit *your* style, and you don't want to waste either your time or theirs on unsuitable work. The UK magazines listed here will sell you a single copy on request. Contact the US magazines and ask if they can also supply single copies.

BOOKS ON WRITING SHORT STORIES

● Donna Baker, *How to Write Stories for Magazines*—the author draws on her own published work and her experience to analyse the popular and more conventional magazine story.

● Michael Baldwin, *The Way to Write Short Stories*—gives plenty of sound advice on plot, character, dialogue and so on. You'll have to dig for the nuggets, though, because the style of writing is idiosyncratic, even occasionally baffling.

● Fay Goldie, *How to Write Stories and Novels that Sell*—discusses what is and what is not commercial, and gives advice on writing saleable material. Don't be put off by the poor production (Malvern's proofreader must have been out-to-lunch that day). Fay Goldie has been writing successfully for 70 years. She's well worth reading.

Four books from the Writer's Workshop series
These are all published by Robinson:

● Orson Scott Card, *Characters & Viewpoint*—clear and comprehensive advice on these vital aspects of fiction writing, including how to select the most effective viewpoint to reveal your characters and develop your plot.

● Ansen Dibell, *Plot*—how to create, develop and sustain gripping storylines, how to balance narration and dramatisation, how to weave plots with sub-plots, and much more.

● Kit Reed, *Revision*—how to revise and rewrite, and improve your narrative skills.

● Lewis Turco, *Dialogue*—how to create believable, natural-sounding dialogue, and how to use dialogue to provide information and move your story along.

And he didn't have to wait till he was President
Everybody, it seems, wants to publish a short story. Abraham Lincoln had his published in the Quincy, Illinois, *Whig* of 15th April 1846. *The Trailor Murder Mystery*, based on a true case, was reprinted in the March 1952 issue of *Ellery Queen's Mystery Magazine*.

9
Your First Novel

GETTING IT RIGHT

Publishers will heap blessings on your head if you can offer an original novel that's in tune with today's markets—better still, tomorrow's.

It can take two or three years to bring a novel from its first assessment to its appearance in the bookshops. Publishers have to be forward-thinking. So does the smart writer. You could be wasting your time trying to catch the coat-tails of yesterday's bestsellers.

The nearest you'll get to a crystal ball is to read *The Bookseller*, especially the fat Spring and Autumn numbers, each of which has about 800 pages of news and information about what is in the pipeline for the coming six months. These special issues cost about £10 each, but if you've made a friend of your local bookseller (and you should) he might let you browse through his copy. The weekly *Publishing News* is helpful, too.

How a success story began

Robert Goddard began his first novel in May 1983, with a rough draft of the plot. Then, over the next six months or so, he put together notes, mostly from his own experience, until he had a 30-page summary of the projected novel. And he began to write.

He completed the first 50 pages and sent them to publishers Robert Hale, whom a friend had recommended. They were interested enough to ask to see the complete novel. It was finished in January 1985. Then came almost a year of assessment, followed by lengthy negotiations about the need to cut the overlong ms, before the contract was signed.

Robert was delighted and amazed that his first novel had been accepted by the first publisher he tried. *Past Caring* was published in 1986. It's a gripping 'I couldn't put it down' story of political and personal intrigue that reaches out from the early years of the century to ensnare characters of the present day. Its publishers regarded it so highly that they nominated it for the Booker Prize.

> Plan your novel thoroughly from beginning to end. Then write 50 or 60 pages of it. Invest in those pages as much energy, creativity and conviction as you can summon. Type them accurately. Package them attractively. Then try them on a publisher or agent. If there is real merit in them, it will be recognised.
>
> Robert Goddard

Since that initial success, Robert Goddard has produced four more novels that have sold widely in both hardback and soft-cover. He also captured quite a few headlines, and doubtless many more readers, when Prime Minister John Major publicly acclaimed him as his favourite author.

BOOKS TO HELP YOU

- Lawrence Block, *Writing the Novel from Plot to Print*—a very readable guide to success, written by an American novelist with more than 100 published novels to his credit. Lawrence Block also wrote the 'Fiction-writing' column in *Writer's Digest* magazine for many years, and helped many authors along the road to success.
- John Braine, *Writing a Novel*—a thoroughly practical exposition of the novelist's craft, regarded as a classic on its subject.
- Oscar Collier with Frances Spatz Leighton, *How to Write and Sell Your First Novel*—American literary agent Collier teams up with freelance writer Leighton to give solid and practical instruction and advice.
- Dianne Doubtfire, *The Craft of Novel-Writing*—practical advice and plenty of illustrative examples of how it's done.
- Paddy Kitchen, *The Way to Write Novels*—shows the skills you need in writing prose fiction.
- Michael Legat, *Writing for Pleasure and Profit*—this excellent all-rounder is particularly good on novel-writing.
- Gary Provost, *Make Every Word Count*—a detailed analysis of how to write richly textured yet concise narrative and dialogue.
- Gordon Wells, *The Book Writer's Handbook*—useful both as a market guide for the first novelist, and as a reference to

established authors seeking new outlets. Look for the latest edition—reference information of this detailed kind can be quickly overtaken by changes in publishers' policies (and ownership).

- Phyllis Whitney, *Guide to Fiction Writing*—one of the most popular writers of romantic suspense-fiction tells you how it's done.

AGENTS

The Dorian Literary Agency, Gregory and Radice, and Diane Burston all handle full length novel mss. Many others are listed in the *Writers' & Artists' Yearbook* and *The Writer's Handbook*.

'GENRE' FICTION

In most of the writers' manuals you'll read, you'll see references to 'genre' or 'category' fiction. Some 'literary' writers and critics tend to use these terms in a slightly derogatory way, but don't let that worry you. It's no more and no less difficult to write a good 'genre' novel than it is to write a good 'general' novel. Publishers often divide novels into 'categories' just for ease of reference. Bear in mind, anyway, that the categories frequently overlap: 'romantic-suspense', 'spy-thriller', 'war-adventure' and so on. You can combine them as you wish.

How could you categorise, for instance, Douglas Adams's *Dirk Gently's Holistic Detective Agency*? *The Bookseller* defined it as 'Ghost-Horror-Detective-Whodunnit-Time-Travel-Romantic-Musical-Comedy'.

Crime and mystery

Most of the major publishers have crime lists, and they'll snap up a good original story, especially if you can create a character or characters who might be ripe for a series. H.R.F. Keating's 'Inspector Ghote', Ruth Rendell's 'Wexford', Reginald Hill's 'Dalziel and Pascoe', Lesley Grant-Adamson's 'Rain Morgan', Jonathan Gash's 'Lovejoy' . . . their sales go up with every new story.

To write modern crime stories successfully, you have to keep up to date with developments in detection methods—genetic finger-printing, for instance, and computerised databanks. You can't afford to get left behind, or to make mistakes. Crime story mss are assessed by experts who will spot any errors or clumsy fudging. Don't risk your credibility by neglecting your research.

On the other hand, don't be so earnest that you forget that you're writing a story that people will read for relaxation and entertainment. You're not in the business of writing forensic textbooks.

The more I think of it the more I come to believe the key to successful fiction writing is always, on every page, with every word, to tell it to your readers. It's what all the great writers did; it's what all the bestselling writers do. Do it too.

H.R.F. Keating, President of the Detection Club

H.R.F. Keating has been writing successful crime stories since the 1960s. He also writes what he calls 'mystery with history', crime novels in a Victorian setting, under the pen-name of Evelyn Hervey. In his book *Writing Crime Fiction* he shares his experience and knowledge of crime novels and crime-writing. His advice and insights on writing will be invaluable to all fiction writers, whatever their preferred genre.

In *Plotting and Writing Suspense Fiction*, Patricia Highsmith discusses her own experience of writing, charting her failures as well as her successes. She claims that the book 'is not a how-to-do-it' handbook, but in fact it's packed with detailed analyses of the techniques of mystery-suspense writing.

And no crime-writer's bookshelf is complete without Julian Symons's *Bloody Murder*, a history of crime-writing from its beginnings to the early 1980s. In the original edition, published in 1972, the author made a series of predictions about likely future trends in crime fiction. In the 1985 edition, he reviews what has actually happened.

Thrills and spies
Thrillers of all kinds are big sellers. Len Deighton, Jack Higgins, Wilbur Smith, Robert Ludlum, Dick Francis all shoot straight into the bestseller lists.

Fast-moving, 'visual' writing works best. Television has conditioned thriller addicts to expect plenty of action. Long descriptive passages that used to be essential for scene-setting are boring to today's readers, who have an enormous storehouse of images in their memories. They don't need explanations of what a computer screen, or a race-course, or even Red Square looks like.

Spy stories have become highly sophisticated—the writing's

better, too. The public's knowledge of computer-hacking for information, 'spy-in-the-sky' satellites and psychiatric drugs has made Ian Fleming's early James Bond 'fairytales-with-gadgets' seem as unreal as *Thunderbirds*. We've grown weary, too, of Le Carré-type 'seedy mutterings behind plywood partitions somewhere off the Charing Cross Road'. *Glasnost* and the demolition of the Berlin Wall, so swiftly followed by the break-up of the Soviet Union, have changed the focus of spy stories for the foreseeable future. Sharp writers moved immediately to a new centre of interest. Look on the bookshop shelves—note how many stories now focus on the Middle East, reviving the centuries-old differences between the West and Islam.

Some publishers with good crime and thriller lists
Constable, Gollancz, HarperCollins, Headline, Robert Hale, Century. The Women's Press publishes feminist crime and thrillers. Espionage is published by Grafton, Simon & Schuster, Hodder & Stoughton, Century, HarperCollins.

Research
If you need specialist research for your crime novel, contact Roderick J. Richards at his agency 'Tracking Line'. A former Head of the West Midlands Police Law Research Unit, Rod specialises in biography and police and criminal history. He offers other services, including ghosting (see p. 169).

Action-adventure
Easy to recognise, but almost impossible to define, an action-adventure story can be set anywhere in the world, in the present or in the past, even in the future, where it crosses boundaries into science fiction.

Fast-moving, full of action and excitement, with plenty of cliff-hangers—these are the essentials. You need to create dynamic characters, fleshed-out and convincing enough to make your reader believe in them for the duration of the story.

Some publishers of action-adventure
Century, Grafton, Gollancz, New English Library, Viking, Bantam, HarperCollins.

Westerns
The Western, on the other hand, is a clearly definable genre.

According to the Western Writers of America, it's a story set in the American West before the 20th century.

If you're interested in Westerns, either writing them or reading them, you could join the J.T. Edson Appreciation Society, which will keep you in contact with other devotees and some practitioners. J.T. Edson, whose books you'll find in profusion on your library and bookshop shelves, is an Englishman who has earned his living by writing Westerns for some years now. He's an authority on the history of the Old West, and a passionate champion of the Western novel.

Like popular romantic fiction, the Western is unjustly regarded with disdain by 'literary' authors and editors. J.T. Edson says he feels he should warn aspiring writers of Westerns that editorial staff, he finds, have been conditioned from early childhood to regard the genre as substandard literature. They're disinclined to believe that an author who specialises in Westerns can possibly write anything else which will prove saleable. If you write, as J.T. does, under your own name, you might find it hard to be taken seriously should you want to break into another genre.

If you're still game to try, Robert Hale and Severn House both have Western lists.

Science fiction
From H.G. Wells to Ray Bradbury, some of the most exciting writing in English literature explores the possibilities of life and intelligence beyond the known frontiers of time and space. Good writers who can supply what this market needs will be welcomed with open cheque books.

If you would like to try, you could join the British Science Fiction Association, which features, among other publications, *Focus*, a magazine for amateur writers.

Interzone magazine, edited by Simon Ounsley and David Pringle, publishes science-fiction short stories, and keeps its readers abreast of all the best that's happening in the world of science-fiction writing.

And there's a book, *Writing Science Fiction* by Christopher Evans.

Some science fiction publishers:
Grafton, Headline, Gollancz (a very strong list), Methuen, Severn House, and The Women's Press, who launched the first ever women's science fiction list.

Fantasy and horror

Don't be tempted to regard this as a 'hack' market. In an article published in 1973 in the American *Writer's Digest*, Stephen King described the genre as 'one of the most delicate known to man and it must be handled with great care and more than a little love'.

Within the accepted rules of good story-telling (that a story should be original, gripping and well-crafted) there are no restrictions. You can make magic, you can set your tale anywhere, anytime, in this world or one of your own making. *The Lord of the Rings* is a fantasy. So is *Superman*.

But remember that a successful fantasy needs its own disciplines. It should be logical within its own terms. And above all it should tell a story. Enchanted lands, elves, monsters, mystery and magic are only elements of a story, not a substitute for it.

If you lean towards the 'horror' side of fantasy, and enjoy reading Stephen King, Brian Lumley, Dean R. Koontz and James Herbert —in other words, if you enjoy having your blood curdled— you'll realise that the most successful horror writers play on our own fears: fear of the dark, of death, of private personal horrors like rats, bats, snakes and spiders, but most of all on our fear of the unknown.

It's an intensely personal genre. To succeed, you need total faith in what you're writing.

> Don't *always* listen to editors, and never listen to friends. A very small number of my works were improved by the suggestions of editors, but just as many have been damaged. Don't deliberately shape your work to another's design; if it's not quite right just now, come back to it when your inner man (woman) has had time to solve the problems. Remember: the road to many a moderate literary success is thick with the ghosts of friendly advice and the dust of dead friendships . . .
>
> Brian Lumley

Join the British Fantasy Society (BFS) which covers the fantasy, horror and science fiction fields. BFS publishes a regular newsletter, a magazine called *Dark Horizons*, and organises an annual Fantasy Conference, Fantasycon.

Some publishers of fantasy and horror stories
Macdonald, New English Library, Headline, Grafton, Severn House.

Romance, romantic-suspense, romantic-historical

Don't skip this bit just because you're a man. Romantic novelists 'Jennifer Wilde' and 'Vanessa Royall' are both men, and Mills & Boon have at least two men among their regular writers. When Mary Wibberley ran a competition for 'the best first hundred words of a romantic novel' in the hardback edition of *To Writers with Love*, the joint first-prize winners both turned out to be men writing under women's names.

There's plenty of help and advice available. Mills & Boon offer an audio cassette from their Reader Service, together with detailed writers' guidelines.

The Romantic Novelists' Association offers membership on a probationary basis, even if you've had nothing published yet.

Books
- Mary Wibberley, *To Writers with Love*—entertaining and challenging, guaranteed to get you writing. Mary specialises in writing for Mills & Boon, and her book is especially useful in its insights into that particular publisher's requirements.
- Jean Saunders, *The Craft of Writing Romance*—covers a wider range of romantic writing, with enlightening contributions from editors and successful writers of the genre.
- Yvonne MacManus, *You Can Write a Romance and Get it Published*—a very helpful book, published in hardback by Severn House and in paperback by Coronet. The Coronet edition has been allowed to go out of print, but there are some copies of the hardback appearing on the 'Creative Writing' shelves in some bookshops. You might also find it in the library.
- Rhona Martin, *Writing Historical Fiction*—covers family sagas, adventure, nostalgia and the 'straight' historical as well as the romantic-historical genre. Good on research, dialogue and language, getting the background right and much else.
- Eric Partridge, *Penguin Dictionary of Historical Slang*— indispensable reference book for writers of historical novels. It will help you avoid those awful anachronisms of speech that crop up in too many otherwise well researched books.

And when you're ready, **a few publishers to try**: Century, Robert Hale, Heinemann, Hodder & Stoughton, Macmillan, and of course Mills & Boon.

10
Writing for Children and Teenagers

Do you have a fund of ideas for stories, informative articles, games, puzzles, jokes and picture-stories? There's plenty of room in the market for all of these—if you can write them really well.

CHILDREN'S BOOKS

Writing for children is a very specialised business. You shouldn't make the mistake, as so many writers do, of assuming that it's easier to write for children than for adults. It isn't. You have to study the markets very closely, and work at developing the right kind of writing techniques. And those techniques will be different for each age group.

There's no room for amateurs here. Publishers receive shoals of stories with enthusiastic covering letters on the lines 'My children loved this when I read it to them—I'm sure others will, too.' Many of these mss arrive complete with unbelievably bad illustrations ('My friend has kindly done the pictures for you. She's always been good at drawing'). Unless your collaborator's work is up to professional standard, this will kill your hopes of publication stone dead. You'll often find, too, that publishers prefer to commission their illustrations from a regular 'stable' of artists whose work is of a type and standard that the publisher knows and trusts.

Writing *and* illustrating a story call for professional skills far beyond the ability to entertain your own or a neighbour's children, but if you think you'd like to investigate the possibility, read Felicity Trotman's book *How to Write and Illustrate Children's Books*.

The success rate in writing for children indicates that the younger the age group, the harder it is to cater for. The more simple and spare the writing, the more skill is needed to get it just right. When you read books on the subject by successful children's writers, you'll see just how complex a discipline it is. Three of the best are *The Way to Write for Children* by Joan Aiken, *Writing for Young Children* by Claudia Lewis, and *How to Write for Children* by Tessa Krailing.

Read these, *then* decide if you could produce the kind of material publishers want. Some teachers believe that many publishers don't really know what children like to read. They could be right, but the writer who wants to get his or her children's book accepted by a publisher has to deliver what that publisher wants. (If you want to pioneer a revolution in children's books you'll probably have to become a publisher yourself.)

It's vital to study the *current* markets. Many writers, especially older ones, tend to submit the kind of stories that were popular when their children (or even they themselves) were young. Their subject matter, language and treatment are inappropriate to today's market.

Spend time in the children's section of the library, and look at *recently* published books, both fiction and non-fiction. Study the various age ranges—note how the vocabulary becomes more challenging as the target age increases. Note the subject matter and treatment.

Don't send work to any publisher without first making a detailed study of their products in the age range and type of book that interests you. Every publishing house strives for a distinct personality and style. *Buy* some of their books, get out your coloured pens, and analyse them down to the last comma. A vague idea of what the publisher needs will not be good enough.

Some publishers of children's books
Andersen Press, Brimax, Blackie Children's Books, Gollancz, HarperCollins, Cape, Dorling Kindersley . . . You'll find many more listed in the *Writers' & Artists' Yearbook* and *The Writer's Handbook*. *The Bookseller* and *Publishing News* will keep you up to date with what's being published.

Games, puzzles, jokes, comic strips
Many puzzle books and comics use freelance material. Look, for example, at D.C. Thomson's *The Beano, The Dandy, Beezer-Topper* and *Twinkle*. Walker Books recently launched a new children's monthly, *Snap*, and if this venture succeeds, other houses might follow. Browse among the comics and puzzle books—do they spark off any ideas?

Almost every paper or magazine uses comic strips. If you're interested in these, either as a potential writer/artist or perhaps as a collector, contact the Association of Comics Enthusiasts, where you'll get plenty of information about comic strips past and present.

For budding authors of comic strips, there's a book that should be useful, *How to Draw and Sell Comic Strips* by Alan McKenzie.

TEENAGE BOOKS

There's been a fast growth in this area over the last few years, with house after house launching new imprints to cater for the 'young adult' market. There are great opportunities here for the writer who can tune in to the adolescent and young teenage wavelengths. You need to be able to write with understanding but without *any* hint of condescension, condemnation or preaching. You need to *like* young people. If today's teenagers horrify, disgust or alarm you, if you don't know street cred from Street-Porter, it's probably better not to try.

Subject matter

Don't shy away from controversial topics. Whether from their own experience or that of their friends, most young people today can identify with such problems as a divorce or death in the family, single parenthood, homelessness, living rough, the generation gap, personal relationships, unemployment, shyness, making sense of the adult world . . . Treated with sensitivity, stories about the problems of daily life as well as traumatic situations can help young adults to understand and come to terms with the darker aspects of life.

Recent titles from Bantam Press, for example, include Joyce Sweeney's *Right Behind the Rain*, the story of a teenage girl's struggles to help her suicidal brother cope with the pressures of success. But on the lighter side the same house published *I Saw Him First*, a romantic comedy by Marjorie Sharmat. The subject scope is as wide as your imagination.

David Silwyn Williams's book *How to Write for Teenagers* will show you how to keep on the right lines for today's markets. Jean Saunders includes a constructive chapter on writing for teenagers in her book *Writing Step by Step*, and Tessa Krailing's book, mentioned earlier, gives sound advice, with perceptive analysis of the problems.

Who publishes teenage books?
You'll find the most up-to-date information in *The Bookseller* and in *Publishing News*. The present volatile state of the publishing industry makes it absolutely vital to keep track of who has merged with whom, who has launched a new imprint, who looks like going out of business . . . Haunt your library and bookshops, to see what could be currently marketable. Check the publishers' names, and note those that publish material that appeals to you. Note, too, the dates of first publication. You don't want to study styles, attitudes and 'in' language that have been 'out' for years.

A few publishers of 'young adult' fiction
Bantam Press, Corgi, Hodder & Stoughton, HarperCollins, Walker Books, The Women's Press, Faber, Virago.

PICTURE-SCRIPTS

Picture stories are stories told in picture form, either drawn or using photographs. The illustrations incorporate text in the form of dialogue in 'balloons', and sometimes in captions in or below the pictures.

D.C. Thomson & Co. Ltd are prolific publishers of picture-script magazines for boys and girls of all ages—*Jackie, Victor, Twinkle* and *Beezer-Topper* are just a few of their titles.

D.C. Thomson will send you, on request, a comprehensive pack of information about writing story scripts, and will encourage and advise you if you show promise in writing the right kind of material for them. Send for the guidelines and study them, then study some of the publications before you send in any material. Every magazine has its own distinctive characteristics, and you'll need to show an awareness of the specific requirements of any that you choose to write for. Stories are not interchangeable among the magazines.

You won't be required to supply the illustrations—these are done by commissioned artists—but you must present your script in such a way that the artist has a clear idea of what you want your readers to see in each picture.

The sample script shows you how this is done. It's the title page of a story from one of D.C. Thomson's girls' papers. You'll see that the speeches have to be very concise. There's no room in the pictures for long explanatory speeches. The text and illustrations work together to move the story along. And don't lose sight of the fact that what you're writing is a *story*, not just a series of scenes.

1—Large heading picture. Leave space for title and the following introductory paragraph—

When Gary and Lesley Stark were orphaned in a road accident, they went to live at Springbank Children's Home.
Gary and Lesley hoped to find a foster family where they could remain together, but had been disappointed so far. One day, Mrs Martin, the house mother, had news of a young couple who wanted to foster the twins—

Picture shows Mrs Martin talking to the twins in her sitting room.
Mrs Martin—*Mr and Mrs Hardy seem a really nice young couple. They love children, but they haven't any of their own, so they'd like you to spend a weekend with them.*
Lesley—*That sounds terrific, Mrs Martin, but Gary and I won't build up our hopes too high. We've had a few disappointments already.*

2—Caption—*But at first, the Hardys did seem to be the perfect foster parents—*
Picture shows Mr and Mrs Hardy, a bright looking couple in their thirties, smiling as they lead the children from their car up the path to a small, neat terrace house with pretty front garden.
Mr Hardy—*We've been really looking forward to this weekend, kids! I hope you like our little house. It's going to be a bit of a tight fit with four people in it, but WE don't mind if YOU don't.*
Lesley—*It looks lovely, Mr Hardy, and we LIKE small houses— they're cosy!*

3—Caption—*Mrs Hardy showed Lesley where she was going to sleep—*
Picture shows Lesley looking puzzled as she looks around small room with nursery furniture in it. The room has clearly been meant for a baby.
Lesley—*Mrs Martin didn't tell me that you had a baby, Mrs Hardy. This room is a nursery, isn't it?*
Mrs Hardy—*Yes it is, Lesley. We did have a little baby of our own years ago, but she died, soon after she was born. We haven't had the heart to change the room since.*

4—Picture shows close-up of Lesley looking thoughtful.
Lesley—*Poor Mrs Hardy. It must have been terrible for her, to lose her baby like that. Let's hope Gary and I will be able to help her forget her sadness.*

5—Caption—*At tea time—*
Picture shows Mrs Hardy serving twins boiled eggs, toast strips and glasses of milk. She and her husband have meat and salad and teapot set in front of them. Lesley is sitting next to Gary, glowering at him.
Mrs Hardy—*Here we are, kiddies—nice eggies with toast soldiers, and lovely milk. If you're good, there will be stewed apple for afterwards.*
Gary—*What! B-but . . . oww!*

6—Picture shows Lesley smiling sweetly at her cross brother.
Gary—*You kicked me, Les. Watch where you're putting your feet.*
Lesley—*Sorry, Gary.*
(Thinks)—*I had to stop him complaining about this baby food Mrs Hardy has made for us.*

7—Caption—*After tea—*
Picture shows Gary and Lesley sitting in living room. The Hardys can be seen washing up in kitchen through the serving hatch.
Gary—*Why did they make that special baby tea for us, when they were having ham salad, Les? Do you think they were trying to save money?*
Lesley—*I expect they thought they were doing us a favour by making us a special meal. Maybe they don't realise ten-year-olds eat the same sort of food as grown ups.*

Figure 13. A sample script
Reproduced by permission of D.C. Thomson & Co. Ltd.

CORRESPONDENCE COURSES

There are specialised correspondence courses in writing for children:

- **The Academy of Children's Writers** offers a tutored course, with written assignments. You can examine the complete printed course material before you commit yourself.
- Arthur Waite, Managing Editor of **Freelance Press Services** runs a tutored course in Children's Authorship.
- **The London School of Journalism** offers a tutored course, Writing for Children.
- **'Written By'** (Vince Powell and George Evans) offer a tutored course in Writing for Children.

The above organisations will send you details and current terms on request. The addresses are in the appendices under Writing Courses, page 171.

11
Writing Poetry, Song Lyrics and Greeting Cards

POETRY

Poetry—the Olympic Games of writing. There's no money in it, unless you're lucky enough to win a big competition, yet the battle for publication and recognition is at its most intense here.

To take just one poetry magazine, *Outposts Poetry Quarterly* receives over 80,000 unsolicited poems every year. There's only space for 50 or so in each issue, but that doesn't stop them flooding in.

How do you get started?

How do you publish your poetry? Where do you start? Firstly you read other people's poetry—both contemporary and classical—sufficient to familiarise yourself with the art so that you know what you are doing. Then research the market—buy poetry books, subscribe to literary magazines. Get a clear picture in your mind of the contemporary scene, and support it, it is the one you wish to join. Finally send some of your own material off for consideration. Always typed and never without a stamped addressed envelope.

Peter Finch

Peter Finch is a poet, editor and writer of both fiction and non-fiction books, with many published volumes to his credit. He runs the Welsh Arts Council's Oriel Bookshop in Cardiff. You should read his book *How to Publish Your Poetry*, a goldmine of practical advice and information that will give you a valuable working knowledge of poetry publishing. Let's look at the points he makes:

Read other people's poetry
Writing good poetry is not just a matter of setting words out in

lines, like chopped-up prose. Poetry editors despair at the lack of craftsmanship displayed by so many would-be poets. You need to know how to combine the various elements of poetry to achieve the effects you want. The only way to do this is to study poetry closely, to analyse how its elements work—sound, rhyming patterns, rhythm, form, all have a part to play. You can learn how to study and analyse poetry from a book like *How Poetry Works* by Philip Davies Roberts.

Research the market
Read what is being published today. Unless you're in touch with current poetry publishing, you can't know what editors are looking for. Too many poets are sadly out of touch. Some even insist on sending verse of the 'Prithee, I come my troth to plight' vintage to contemporary poetry magazines. It isn't that editors only want 'modern' or experimental poetry. Far from it. Good contemporary poetry takes many forms. But editors still receive hopelessly archaic verse sent by poets who seem to have read nothing written this side of the Boer War.

Get to know the magazines you like, and support them
Every poetry magazine has its own distinctive flavour. When you find one whose poetry is in tune with your own preferences, concentrate on that magazine, at least to begin with. Don't even consider sending your poetry to a magazine you don't feel comfortable with, or in which you wouldn't be proud to be published. And don't send anything to a magazine you haven't seen—you don't know what kind of company you might be courting.

Subscribe to at least one magazine, more if you can afford it. It's in your own long-term interest to help keep the poetry scene alive. You need these magazines as much as they need you.

When you're ready to try for publication
Present your work as shown in the example on page 135, typed, single-spaced with the stanzas clearly divided, and only one poem, however short, to a page.

Put your name and address on every sheet—on the back if you prefer. Anne Lewis-Smith, former editor of *Envoi*, says she published several poems that arrived without identification, and kept hoping that their authors would contact her to claim their entitlement of complimentary copies. (*Envoi* is now edited by Roger Elkin—See page 139.)

Unborn Children

These ghosts haunt differently, they come before,
Slowly, like secrets, pointing empty sleeves
From the margins of life, and promise more
Than the pattern anticipation weaves;
Some day I'll hear their laughter and their cries,
Touch their small hands and kiss their sleeping eyes.

They sing their coming in a swelling life,
The pleasure of our bodies' creating,
A helpless immortality my wife
And I can only tremble for, waiting
Until we hear their laughter and their cries,
Touch their small hands and kiss their sleeping eyes.

They are my laughter at the frightened years
When pain was loneliness and solitude,
My freedom from my generation's tears,
A promise of a sure familiar mood
When I hear their laughter and their cries,
Touch their small hands and kiss their sleeping eyes.

                                        Mike Pattinson

'Unborn Children' was published in *Acumen* magazine in October 1986, and is reproduced here in typescript form with Mike Pattinson's permission.

Never send anything (even an enquiry) without an SAE. And please don't ask for free copies 'to see if I like your magazine' or 'to study your requirements'. Small magazines struggle along on tiny budgets. Very few make even a marginal profit. You shouldn't expect them (or any other markets, for that matter) to subsidise your market study and your postage.

How to save money, time and aggravation
● Don't submit work to major publishing houses. A few, like Faber & Faber, do publish poetry, but say that they seldom find that a beginner's work meets their standards. Wait till you have a respectable number of poems in print before you think

about a collection. And it's totally pointless to send single poems to big publishers.

- Don't send poetry to magazines that never publish it. They won't make an exception for you, however good you are.

- Don't send a saga the length of 'The Anglo-Saxon Chronicle' to a small magazine where it would fill a whole issue.

- Never send the same poem to more than one magazine at a time. This is known as 'multiple submission', and will do your reputation no good at all. You risk a double acceptance—not the triumph you might think. The editors concerned will be mutually embarrassed, and won't forgive you easily. Don't imagine they won't find out. Poetry editors see a lot of poetry magazines, and even if they didn't see the gaffe for themselves, you can be sure some indignant poet will 'advise' them.

POETRY 'ON THE AIR'

Poet Peggy Poole is Poetry Consultant to BBC Network North-west's programme *Write Now*, a weekly half-hour of poems and stories from the region. Peggy has written the following guidelines for you, from her experience of selecting poems suitable for reading 'on the air':

Outlets

If your local BBC or independent radio stations have no poetry programme, ask for one and organise area support. Station managers need persuading that poetry is an active part of life today; many still regard it as 'soft' or childish and think in terms of doggerel. But they will change their minds given evidence of a successful programme which involves local listeners.

Submissions

Submit as for a top-class magazine, with an SAE. Keep poems relatively short—a rough line limit of 40. (This does not mean the total exclusion of any longer work, particularly of a possible dramatic poem for several voices. In such a case it would be wise to write to the producer in advance explaining the content, and a decision will be made either to present an extra, one-off programme or to vary the style of the regular poetry programme for that one special occasion.)

Do not use four-letter words even if they are an integral part of a poem; this will jeopardise the programme.

Keep off politics, and ensure seasonal work arrives with plenty of time in hand. Humour is welcomed provided it is genuinely poetic and does not belong to a comedy programme. It's best to avoid nostalgic or pseudo-religious poems—huge amounts of these are received, but hardly ever used. Religious poems belong to religious programmes and, with a region of such variety, one person's nostalgia, unless of real quality, becomes someone else's boredom.

Reading

Many poets want to read their own work, but studios at the average broadcasting station are usually too heavily booked for this to be possible. It will depend on the producer and the length and format of the programme.

Payment

Do not expect this to be more than a token payment.

> A good poem should work as well on radio as in print, but it is important to remember that your audience is probably engaged in several other occupations while listening, so your poem needs to work instantly at one level while offering resonances of deeper meaning at the same time. For many years in producing BBC Radio Merseyside's poetry programme, I balanced on a tightrope, aiming both to attract the established poet without intimidating new poets from submitting their first attempts, and to present an enjoyable half-hour that might also succeed in converting a newcomer to poetry. Now, choosing poetry for *Write Now*, there is also the nature of the region to consider.
>
> Peggy Poole

Study this market, too

Listen to as much broadcast poetry as you can. At the time of writing, the BBC is in the throes of a 'shake-up' of sound broadcasting, and their future policy on poetry is not yet clear. Details of poetry programmes are given every week in *Radio Times*. Local radio details are given for your region as a group. *Write Now* is broadcast at different times and on different days on BBC Radio Merseyside, BBC Radio Lancashire, Greater Manchester Radio and BBC Radio Cumbria.

Do try to listen to the programme even if your work is not being broadcast that week.

Checklist for poetry submissions
1. Each poem is typed in the accepted form on a separate sheet of plain white A4 paper.
2. Your name and address appear on every sheet.
3. You've kept a note of where you're sending each poem, so that you don't risk a multiple submission, and kept a copy of each poem submitted.
4. You haven't sent more than six poems at any one time.
5. You've enclosed a stamped self-addressed envelope big enough and bearing adequate postage for the return of the whole batch.

Send your work either to Jenny Collins, Producer, 'Write Now', or to Peggy Poole, at BBC Network Northwest, P.O. Box 693, Liverpool L69 3NW.

SOURCES OF INFORMATION AND ADVICE

- **The Association of Little Presses** (ALP) issues *Poetry and Little Press Information* (PALPI), and a current catalogue of *Little Press Books in Print*.
- **The Friends of the Arvon Foundation** produce a regular newsletter of information about competitions, festivals, writers' markets and literature.
- **The National Poetry Foundation** offers to members news of competitions and publications, and runs a poetry appraisal service for members.
- **The Oriel Bookshop** publishes *Small Press and Little Magazines of the UK and Ireland* (a regularly updated address list), a catalogue of recent poetry publications, a regular programme of literary events, a mail order 'books on books' service, and *for writers living in Wales only*, a criticism service subsidised by the Welsh Arts Council.
- **The Poetry Society** issues *Poetry Review Quarterly*, and also an information bulletin, advance notification of all Poetry Society events, access to special offers from the Poetry Society Bookshop, and a criticism service which anyone can use, although society members get reduced rates.
- **The Poetry Book Society** (a book club) offers a *Quarterly*

Bulletin, a free annual *Poetry Anthology*, and discount prices on quality poetry books.

Books

- Peter Finch, *How to Publish your Poetry*—probably the best investment you could make, full of information and practical advice.
- Alison Chisholm, *How to Write Poetry*—this much-published prize-winning poet takes you through the process of writing poetry, from the first spark of an idea to the final revision. Thoroughly practical, detailed discussion and advice.
- Philip Davies Roberts, *How Poetry Works*—explains the ways in which the various elements of English poetry—language, rhythm and metre, rhyming patterns and so on—contribute to a poetic work.

Magazines

Here are a few titles to introduce you to the wide range published. As you become familiar with the poetry scene you'll discover many more—most magazines carry reviews of other publications both established and new.

- *Acumen.* Two issues a year. Well produced and printed. Publishes poetry, prose, reviews, interviews, articles on poets and poetry. 100 plus pages. Editor Patricia Oxley has no preferences on form or content, but you should avoid clichéd subjects.
- *Envoi.* Three issues a year. In 1991, the editorship moved to Roger Elkin, after many years of success with Anne Lewis-Smith. Roger plans fairly extensive changes in editorial policy, including more comprehensive criticism of subscribers' work. For the latest information and current subscription rates, contact Roger Elkin at the address given in the appendices.
- *First Time.* Published twice a year. Neatly printed production, devoted to new poetry by new poets. Editor Josephine Austin.
- *Outposts Poetry Quarterly.* Professionally produced and printed. Publishes a broad range of poetry by both new and established poets, also news and reviews. Now edited by Roland John, following more than 40 years under the stewardship of its founder, the late Howard Sergeant MBE.
- *Stand.* An international quarterly of new writing, publishing new poetry, fiction, plays, translations, criticism and art, and

reviews of new poetry and fiction. Left of centre, and 'hospitable to a wide range of work. Free from prejudice, but socially conscious', the editors' promise. They look for well made but exploratory writing. Lots of advertisements and information about literary publications. Editors Jon Silkin and Lorna Tracy.

● *Writers' Own Magazine*. Duplicated production. Poetry and prose, much of the content is by new or relatively new writers. Some news and reviews. A readers' letters section mostly providing mutual encouragement for its contributors. A useful starting point for beginners. Editor Eileen M. Pickering.

● *The Writers' Rostrum*. Also a duplicated production. Poetry and prose, mostly by new writers. News and reviews, and occasional articles about writers and writing. Very friendly. Editor Jenny Chaplin.

SONGWRITING

Do you dream of writing a 'standard', another 'White Christmas' or 'Stardust'? Did you watch the 'Song for Europe' contest and think 'I could write something better myself'? And maybe you could. From folk to rap, from traditional to pop, there's always room for a good new song.

You can't write music?
You don't have to. What you need is a collaborator. You write the lyrics, your collaborator writes the music, and you take equal shares of any profits.

Look out for sharks
The 'shark' is the music business's equivalent of the vanity publisher. He asks for payment to write music to your lyrics. Don't fall for this. There hasn't yet been a successful song produced in that way. You'd be throwing your money away.

So how do you get started?
You can join a professional organisation, even if you're an absolute unpublished beginner. You'll have access to sound *professional* advice and guidance. If you need a collaborator, you'll be helped to find one who will work with you, on equal terms, with no money changing hands in either direction unless and until your song makes a profit.

'Somebody called Lloyd Webber wants to talk to you.'

The British Academy of Songwriters, Composers and Authors (BASCA) offers Associate Membership to unpublished songwriters. (Please note that the 'Authors' in the name refers to lyric-writers.) Membership costs around £16 per annum. For this, members have access to BASCA's advice and guidance services, and receive a quarterly information bulletin, *BASCA News*. For full details of BASCA membership and services contact the General Secretary at the address given in Associations and Societies Open to Unpublished Writers, page 162.

The Guild of International Songwriters & Composers offers full membership to both amateur and professional songwriters. Services to members include song assessments, collaboration between lyric-writers and composers (the Guild keeps a register of collaborators), information on music publishers' requirements, advice on copyright, contracts and so on. Members receive a free quarterly magazine, *Songwriting and Composing*. Membership costs £20 per annum in the UK, £25 per annum overseas. Contact the Chairman, Roderick G. Jones, at the address given in Associations and Societies Open to Unpublished Writers. The Guild of International Songwriters & Composers has an associated music publishing company, **First Time Music (Publishing) UK Ltd**, at the same address.

And there are books

- Stephen Citron, *Songwriting*—takes you step by step through writing a song, illustrated with words and music from well-known songs. Full of ideas and tricks of the trade, it's particularly helpful for beginners. Covers lyrics, music, rhythm, rhyme, form and style.
- Sheila Davis, *The Craft of Lyric Writing*—a guide to the art of writing words for and to music. Works through examples, and shows how to avoid common pitfalls.

GREETING CARDS

This is where you scout around your newsagent's again, but now you're interested in his display of greeting cards. Greeting cards are very big business. According to recent figures from America, their citizens send out over 10,000,000 'conventional' greeting cards *every day of the year*. And 'conventional' cards are only one category of the six basic types of card. The others are 'informal', 'juvenile', humorous', 'studio' and 'inspirational'.

There's an expanding market here in the UK, too, and quite a few of the card companies buy ideas from freelance writers.

Take time to study the cards. Could you write the kind of copy they use? Many companies print their address, and sometimes a telephone number, on the back of their cards. Contact them to ask if they issue guidelines for copywriters, or, if they don't, whether they have any preferences with regard to presentation. Some companies are very specific about this, others don't mind so long as the ideas are laid out clearly. If there are no instructions about this, it's best to type one idea per sheet of paper, with your name and address on every sheet.

If a company likes the kind of work you send them, even if they don't buy anything right away, they'll probably add your name to their list of copywriters and will send you regular details of their current requirements—seasonal submissions vary from company to company.

At present, your best chance of selling is in the humorous lines. Study each company's cards closely. While at first glance many of the lines appear quite similar, analysis will show that every company has its own style. Here's an idea that was bought from the author by Hanson White Ltd, reproduced here with their permission. (You'll almost invariably be required to sell all rights to your greeting card copy—very few companies pay on a royalty basis.)

Mother's Day:

| Page 1 | You're a Mum in a million. Thanks for putting up with all the naughty things I've done . . . |
| Page 3 | . . . Good job you don't know about the rest!! Happy Mother's Day |

The card made from this idea, illustrated by a commissioned artist, won the 'Mother's Day Best Humorous/Cute Card' category in the 1991 Greetings Industry Spring Awards. It's a good example of a very 'sendable' card which would appeal to a wide range of buyers. The judges said they 'could all relate to it'.

Rates of payment vary, but most companies pay from £25 upwards for each idea bought (some pay much more). You'll find information about American greeting card markets in the American *Writer's Market* which you can get from Freelance Press Services or through bookshops from Harrap Publishing Group.

For UK markets, your best source of information, besides the cards themselves, is the bi-monthly *Greetings*, the magazine of the Greeting Card and Calendar Association—see Information services and sources. You'll find some addresses of UK companies (including Hanson White-Accord) under Greeting Card Companies on page 176.

12
Writing for Radio, Screen and Stage

RADIO AND TELEVISION

The British Broadcasting Corporation (BBC) is one of the
biggest potential markets for freelance writers. Radios Three and
Four broadcast around 500 plays a year between them, and around
50 of these will be written by new writers. Since the axing in 1991
of the radio and television script units, there is now no specific
way of getting your material looked at, so your best plan is to study
the work of producers whose work and choice of material appeals
to you, and send your script (with an SAE) to the producer c/o
the programme at the address of the radio station or TV channel.
Radio Five, the new network for educational and youth programmes, looks for material suitable for children and young people.
Ask for details from the Head of Drama, Radio Five, Broadcasting
House, London W1A 1AA.

Short stories for radio
The recent scheduling changes on BBC Radio Four have resulted
in the best-known short story spot, *Morning Story* being dropped.
There is now, however, an afternoon *Storytime* slot, for which
short stories are needed. The flavour of stories used recently in
Morning Story has been distinctly different from the general rather
bland stories that made up most of its previous content. The stories
that are wanted now for *Storytime* should deal with current issues,
contemporary themes and topical concerns, reflecting the times
and conditions in which we live. The required length is as before,
2,300-2,500 words.

Radio drama
The **Radio Drama Department** broadcasts plays, adaptations,

series and serials. You can get a free leaflet, *Notes on Radio Drama*, from the Literary Manager (Radio Drama) at Broadcasting House —you can also send submissions addressed to the Literary Manager, if you wish.

Radio Light Entertainment

A lot of freelance material is used by topical programmes like *Week Ending* and *The News Huddlines*. Both these programmes hold weekly writers' meetings during their run, and any writer is welcome to attend. The meetings are held at Broadcasting House, Langham Place. You can get information about when the meetings are held by ringing (071) 580 4468 and asking for the production office of the show you're interested in.

Light Entertainment Radio is also interested in scripts or ideas for series, half-hour sit-coms and panel games, mainly for Radios Two and Four. There's a leaflet available on request.

Local radio

There could be openings for all kinds of material on your local radio stations, both BBC and independent. The only way to find out what kind of material might be suitable is to listen in. If you think you can offer something particularly suitable, contact the station manager. Both the *Writers' & Artists' Yearbook* and *The Writer's Handbook* carry comprehensive lists of addresses, the latter giving detailed information about personnel.

Television Drama

BBC TV is interested in original 60-minute plays and 90-minute screen-plays dealing with contemporary themes. The fewer the locations and the smaller the casts needed, the greater your advantage. This is a difficult market to penetrate, and if you're totally unknown your script might be returned unread. Best to make your mark in radio first—see Wally K. Daly's remarks on page 146.

Television Light Entertainment

All submissions for sketch shows like *Smith and Jones*, *The Russ Abbot Show* and so on are considered—you don't need a track record to succeed here if you can supply the right kind of material. You need to study the shows very closely—a video recorder is essential here—and you need to send your material at the appropriate time. A call to the **Comedy Script Unit** will give you information about deadlines.

The **Comedy Department** also seeks new 30-minute series, studio-based in the main for preference. They want to see original formats rather than rehashing of existing programmes.

Scripts and enquiries should be addressed to the Comedy Script Unit, Room 4010, Television Centre, Wood Lane, London W12 7RJ. Tel: (081) 576 1900.

Starting out

If you have no track record don't start by writing for TV drama, *except for fun*—you'd have more chance of winning the pools than having your play bought and transmitted.

The best market for new playwrights is without a doubt BBC Radio. The best slot length is half-hour, followed by *Afternoon Theatre* (45 or 55 minutes).

If you are an intellectual giant write half-hour plays for Radio 3, they are always desperate for a good product.

If you have a sense of humour let it show in your scripts. 'Funny' is more saleable than 'Doom and Gloom'.

Don't waste time entering competitions—back to winning the pools again—simply send your first script, typed, double spaced, A4 paper, good sized left margin, off to BBC Script Unit*, BBC, Broadcasting House, London W1A 1AA, then get on with writing the next. No point in waiting to see how they like the first—it's going to be three months before you hear about that one, unless it's an absolute 'no-no' when it will be back in two.

The only book on the subject I would advise buying is *Writing for the BBC*, a BBC publication that gives all available markets, plus demonstration layout.

See—easy, isn't it?

Wally K. Daly, former Chair, Writers' Guild of Great Britain, writer of drama and television comedy for both radio and TV; also of five stage plays and three musicals, the best known being *Follow the Star* (music, Jim Parker).

Is the money good?

Yes, it can be very good, especially if you can establish yourself as a valued regular contributor. What you'll be paid depends on how

*Note: The BBC Script Unit no longer exists—see page 144.

well established you are. At the time of writing, fees for a short story specially written for radio range from £102 for 15 minutes. The rates for two performances of radio drama (other than educational) are £34.61 per minute for beginners, £52.70 per minute for established writers. You should check current rates of pay with the BBC.

The Comedy Writers Association (CWA)

The Comedy Writers Association was formed in the early 1980s to promote good comedy writing and to encourage and advise new writers. CWA members sell to radio and TV outlets worldwide. They're helped by the lively exchange of experiences, techniques and market information.

Writing saleable comedy material is a very specialised discipline. You have to know what's wanted where and at the right time.

> Every comedian has his own style. Study that style and tailor your work to suit. For example, a joke written for Ken Dodd would be no good for Roy Walker. In situation comedy, keep characters and sets to a minimum. Avoid too much outside filming. Study TV programmes and comedians. And accept rejections—they're part of every comedy writer's life.
>
> Ken Rock, President, Comedy Writers Association

If you'd like to know more about the Comedy Writers Association, contact Ken Rock at the CWA address given in the appendices.

Don't leave it all to the men

Why do most women assume that only men can write funny material? You'll probably find it quite hard to think of more than a handful of women who have made their mark in comedy writing. Victoria Wood, of course, Carla Lane, French and Saunders . . . but not many more.

> For centuries women have laughed at jokes told and written by men. Yet despite being successful as writers, few women attempt to write comedy. Being a keen observer of human nature, seeing the funny side of life and the ability to study comedy writing techniques are not exclusive to men.
>
> Joyce Lister

Joyce Lister has built a successful second career as a comedy writer, after illness forced her to give up her nursing activities. She has sold material to (among other outlets) *The Grumbleweeds* (Granada TV), *Fast Forward* (BBC2 for children), Little and Large and Radio Luxembourg. She achieved her first success with a series of humorous articles based on her nursing experience, published in her local paper. She's also a talented and successful writer of greeting card material. Have you got Joyce's kind of talent? She would like to see many more women writing in these fields.

A specialist service

Rosemary Horstmann, author of *Writing for Radio*, brings her long experience and expertise as a producer, broadcaster, scriptwriter, journalist, tutor and administrator to a service designed to give constructive advice and supportive encouragement to authors who want to write for broadcasting.

Rosemary offers script evaluation, coaching in interviewing techniques, and tuition in the use of a professional tape recorder and the editing of tape. Tuition sessions on scriptwriting and her other services can be arranged either one-to-one or on a group basis. Contact Rosemary for details of services and current charges.

Recommended reading

- *Writing for the BBC*, published by the BBC itself.
- William Ash, *The Way to Write Radio Drama*. Written by a very experienced BBC script editor, and covers the whole field of radio drama.
- Brad Ashton, *How to Write Comedy*. A practical and entertaining guide to writing saleable comedy, from one-liners to situation comedy. (Required reading for intending CWA members.)
- Stewart Bronfield, *Writing for Film and Television*. A step-by-step guide to writing a professional-quality film or television script, written by a veteran producer-writer.
- Phillippa Giles and Vicky Licorish (Eds), *Debut on Two: A Guide to Writing for Television*. Published by the BBC, specifically to encourage new writers and new forms of writing for television drama. Contains advice from successful writers and producers, plus the scripts of the eight plays commissioned following the nationwide *Debut on Two* campaign to discover new television writers.
- Rosemary Horstmann, *Writing for Radio*. Practical advice from a very experienced producer, writer, tutor and lecturer.

- Gerald Kelsey, *Writing for Television*. One of the practical A. & C. Black writers' guides series.
- William Miller, *Screenwriting for Narrative Film and Television*. Narrative structures, settings and dialogue, with examples from well known screenplays.
- Lew Schwartz, *The Craft of Writing TV Comedy*. One of the Allison & Busby writers' guides series.
- William Smethurst, *How To Write For Television*. The complete guide to breaking into this lucrative market.
- *The Stage and Television Today*.

WRITING FOR FILM AND VIDEO

Most film and video companies will only look at material submitted through an established agent. You could try contacting one of the agents listed in the *Writers' & Artists' Yearbook* and *The Writer's Handbook*. Make sure you choose only those who specify an interest in this field. Your chances are slim, however, unless you can present some reasonably impressive work-in-progress and preferably also a portfolio of published work. They're not really likely to be interested in a total beginner.

As a newcomer, your best first move is to send for details of the **London Screenwriters Workshop**. Although this association is based in London, it caters for many out-of-town and overseas members, too. And you don't need any track record to join.

WRITING FOR THE STAGE

Your best starting point as a new playwright is a local repertory theatre or amateur dramatic group. If you have no track record at all, it's unrealistic to expect to see your name in lights in London's West End with your first effort. Not impossible, but not likely.

However, management companies send scouts to repertory productions all over the country. They're always on the lookout for original and potentially profitable plays, and yours might be 'spotted'.

It's usually best to write first and ask if the company would like to see your script. Give all the relevant details: type of play, how many sets, how many characters and so on.

Never send anyone your only copy.

Read up on production contracts *before* you sign any agreement. *The Writers' & Artists' Yearbook* explains contracts in detail.

Well, you can dream, can't you?

Playwrights' groups

Ask your nearest Regional Arts office (phone numbers and addresses are in the *Writers' & Artists' Yearbook*) for details of any **playwrights' association** in your area. Most of these groups hold readings and can arrange for script criticism.

The **Player-Playwrights** society reads, performs and discusses plays and scripts, to help members improve and market their work.

Membership of the **New Playwrights' Trust (NPT)** is open to all playwrights, aspiring playwrights, and those interested in developing and encouraging new playwriting. There are workshops, a script-reading service, a writer/company Link Service and a monthly newsletter.

The **Theatre Writers' Union** specialises in the concerns of all who write for live performance. It has a nationwide network, and membership is open to every playwright who has written a play, performed or not.

Getting your play published

It's well worth trying to get your play published, especially if it's been considered good enough to be given live performance by a local company. You can send your script to **Samuel French Ltd**, who publish nothing else but plays. If French's publish it, they'll include it in their *Guide to Selecting Plays*, a substantial catalogue of plays intended for performance by amateur dramatic groups.

You don't need an agent to approach French's, but they prefer that the play should have been tried out in some kind of performance, because that reveals flaws that might have been overlooked in the written work, and which you could correct before submitting the piece for professional consideration. They make no assessment charge. French's will send you, on request and free of charge, their mail order lists of books and cassettes on all the media and performing arts: writing, acting, production, make-up and so on, from Shakespeare to pantomime. (It helps if you can specify your area or areas of interest.)

Theatre production companies

You could try making direct contact with some of the dozen or so professional production companies who actively seek new writers' work. There's a useful section on theatre companies in *The Writer's Handbook*. Stick to companies who specify an interest in new writing.

Specific requirements

Production companies, like book and magazine publishers, have their own individual styles and requirements. Very few plays would suit them all. Find out as much as you can about a company's preferences before you approach them. This groundwork could pay good dividends. Study the entries in *The Writer's Handbook*, and read *The Stage and Television Today*. These will give you a good idea of what production companies are interested in.

Read the small ads in *The Stage and Television Today*, where you'll sometimes find small companies asking for scripts.

When you send a script to a production company, use the standard layout. Make it quite clear who is saying what, and which lines are speech and which are stage directions. Study the sample script on page 152, an extract from Steve Wetton's play *King of the Blues*.

Steve also offers you this tip: Nowadays, directors and actors tend to fall about laughing when they see the kind of detailed stage directions that used to litter playscripts. Directions like 'Jeremy moves downstage right, knocks his pipe out in the ashtray to the left of the paperweight and then goes to lean nonchalantly with his right elbow on the shelf above the mantelpiece' are a total giveaway of a writer's inexperience.

There's a helpful booklet you can send for, *The Playscript from Scratch*, compiled by David Huxley. It's a beginner's guide to

ACT ONE   SCENE 4

*(Into Daniel's fantasy) The stage remains in
total darkness for a few seconds. Then we hear
a voice off. It is Daniel's own voice but
distorted and amplified to sound God-like.*

VOICE: In the beginning there was the stadium. But the
                stadium was empty and the ground without
                shape or form.

                *There is a roll of thunder and a flash of lightning
                lights up the stage for a second. We see a
                deserted football stadium.*

                Darkness was everywhere. Then the spirit of
                God moved in the wilderness and said: Let
                there be light.

                *Lights up. But they are floodlights as at a
                football stadium.*

                This was the first day and it was good. But
                God saw that the stadium was empty and the
                gates were poor so he didst command: Upon
                these terraces let there come forth all creatures
                great and small.

                Football fans enter. Bewildered at first. Newly born.

                And he called these creatures *(pause)* fans.

                *Explosion of noise. Cheering etc. It stops as suddenly
                as it began.*

                Then God blessed these creatures and said unto
                them: Go forth and multiply.

FAN: He said what?

VOICE   You heard. Go forth and multiply.

FAN: Right, lads. Let's get at it. *(They try)*

VOICE: And this was the second day and it was good.
                (Pause) But not *that* good for he had not yet
                invented women. *(Groans from fans)*

FANS: *(Chant)* Why are we waiting? Why are we
                waiting . . . ?

Figure 14. Example of how to set out a play script
© Steve Wetton. Reproduced with permission. From Steve Wetton's
play *King of the Blues*, performed at the Derby Playhouse. Not yet
published.

preparing and marketing a script, with explanations and examples of the accepted playscript format, and information about copyright, study courses, grants, literature and more.

Grants and bursaries

The Arts Council of Great Britain gives details of various forms of financial assistance in their brochure *Theatre Writing Schemes.* For a copy of the brochure and further information, contact the Drama Director, The Arts Council of Great Britain.

Some companies to approach

Here are the detailed requirements of three companies who welcome new playscripts:

Paines Plough, The Writers' Company
Produces nothing but new writing. A Readers' Panel reports on all scripts submitted (this can take two or three months). They offer you the following tips about submitting scripts:

- *Do* take care with the layout. It's especially important to distinguish between dialogue and stage directions. Underline all stage directions *or* type them in capitals.
- *Do* put the full name of the character (not an initial or other abbreviation) in capitals on the left hand side of the page before every speech. Spread out generously. *Never* use both sides of the paper.
- *Do* enclose a suitably sized SAE.
- *Do* include a brief synopsis, fewer than 200 words.
- *Do* make the cover of the play look interesting in some way.
- *Don't* send more than one play at a time. The envelopes that collect most dust are the ones containing 'a selection' of the author's work. Find out about the company you're writing to and send them the play you think most appropriate—if they want more, they'll ask for more.
- *Don't* say too much in your covering letter. Avoid a detailed explanation of your play's themes and meaning—if these are not clear in the play itself, then you've written it badly.
- *Don't* waste a fortune in postage. Send out a synopsis with a sample scene, and find out which companies are really interested.
- *Don't* pester people. Wait at least three months before enquiring about a response.

The Traverse Theatre, Edinburgh
One of the country's foremost producers of unknown work by new writers. They read everything that comes in, but say it helps if authors observe a few basic requirements:

- *Do* limit the cast to not more than nine characters. Include a character list and the number of actors required.
- *Do* include a line or two on the setting ('London in the Blitz', 'contemporary living room' and so on).
- *Do* remember that small underfunded theatres like the Traverse can't do spectacular effects with swimming pools, live animals and the like.
- *Do* note that the company looks for plays that say something new. There would be little interest in scripts about mid-life crises set in kitchen and living room, for example.
- *Do* please use some kind of binding. Readers take piles of scripts home to read—and loose scripts don't mix with children and pets.

Any play you submit to the Traverse Theatre should not have been performed professionally before. Send the full script, not a synopsis.

You'll receive a reader's report from a panel of directors, actors, writers and academics. This can take up to three months, so be patient. Perhaps one author in 20 will be asked to see them. One in 500 might get a workshop reading, and one in 1,000 a full production. If your play is thought to be good but not suitable for the Traverse, they'll advise you about other possible outlets.

The Liverpool Playhouse
Has an active policy of promoting new work in both its auditoria, the Mainhouse which seats 750 (it's an old music-hall theatre), and the Studio, which seats 100 and works to any configuration.

The Playhouse looks for exciting, innovative work from new playwrights, 'the voice of the 90s', with a real feeling of truth in the writing. The company is particularly supportive to local writers through workshops and writer surgeries. These are a few guidelines:

- All new scripts are welcome. They are read by a pool of readers who then submit reports to the Associate Director.

- Scripts can be sent straight to the theatre—no letter or synopsis is required. Everything should be very clearly addressed.
- Scripts should be typed, with all pages numbered.
- There are no stipulated criteria in terms of content, cast, size and so on, but huge casts are difficult.

Recommended reading

French's Theatre Bookshop will send you a list of books relevant to writing for the theatre. In the Elm Tree series there's Tom Gallacher's *The Way to Write for the Stage*, which covers advice about the choice of subject, the action of the play, its structure, using the stage, dialogue, rehearsal, contracts, agents, adaptations and so on.

How to Write a Play for the Amateur Stage by Dilys Gater is a recent addition to the Allison & Busby writers' guides series.

Glossary

Advance A sum paid to an author in advance of publication of his book. The usual terms are that the publisher will retain the author's royalty until the advance is paid off, after which the author receives his agreed share of the profits.

Agreement See **Contract**.

Anthology A collection of stories, poems and so on, which may or may not have been published before.

Article A piece of prose writing that deals with a single subject (less commonly with several related subjects).

Autobiography A person's life story, written by himself.

Balloon A balloon- or bubble-shaped outline containing text.

Bi-monthly Every two months.

Biography A person's life as investigated and evaluated by someone else.

Blurb Promotional text on the flap of a book jacket or the outside back cover of a paperback, sometimes exaggerating its worth.

Bullet A large dot preceding and adding emphasis to an item in a book or article. Also called a stab point.

Byline A line at the head or foot of a piece of writing identifying the writer: 'by Adam Ampersand'.

C A symbol signifying that a work is protected by copyright.

'Category' fiction Fiction written to fit into a specific genre: romance, Western, thriller and so on.

Collaboration The working together of two or more people to produce a work, sometimes published under a single pseudonym. (For example, 'Ellery Queen' who is/are Frederic Dannay and Manfred B. Lee.)

Contract A signed document, an agreement between publisher and author specifying in exact detail the responsibilities each party undertakes in the writing, production and marketing of a book, in terms of payment, assignation of rights and so on.

Copy Matter to be typeset. Usually refers to the prepared typescript.

Copyright The exclusive right in his own work of an author or other designated party, as defined by law.

Copywriting Writing material for use in advertisements, publicity material and the like.

Critique A critical examination and written report on a work.

Deadline The latest date or time by which a job must be finished.

Draft A preliminary version.

Edition One printing of a book. A second or subsequent edition will have alterations, sometimes substantial, compared to the previous edition.

Editorial policy The editor's overall concept of the kind of publication he wants to produce.

FBSR First British Serial Rights. The right to publish a story or article for the first time and once only in the UK. Not applicable to books.

Feature A magazine or newspaper piece, an article which is not one of a series.

Fiction Writing that is not and does not pretend to be truth, but which is entirely drawn from the imagination.

Flyer A leaflet sent out in the post.

Folio 1. A leaf, that is, two pages of a book. 2. A page number. 3. A manuscript page.

'Freebie' A slang term for a freesheet, a publication distributed free to householders, travellers, etc. Anything given without charge.

Freelance A self-employed person who sells his or her services or written work to a publisher for an agreed fee. A writer/journalist who sells work to various publications but is not employed by any one publisher. (Derives from the mercenary knights and soldiers who wandered Europe after the Crusades, hiring out their services, complete with lances, wherever they could.)

Genre A literary species or specific category, for example Westerns, detective stories, etc.

Ghosting/ghost-writing Writing a book in conjunction with someone else (usually a celebrity but could be anyone with a saleable story) as if it had been written by that other person, with no credit given to the writer.

GSM Grammes per square metre (grammage), the specification of paper weights.

Hack A slightly derogatory term applied to a person who writes primarily for money.

HB Abbreviation for 'hardback', a book with a stiff cover.

Imprint 1. The name of the printer with the place and time of printing, required by law in many countries for papers, books and so on meant for publication. 2. The name of the publisher with place and date of publication.

IRC International Reply Coupon, a voucher sold at post offices worldwide, equivalent to the value of the minimum postal rate for a letter posted in the country from which the reply will come.

ISBN International Standard Book Number, a unique ten-digit reference number given to every book published, to identify its area of origin, publisher, title and check control.

ISSN International Standard Series Number, an eight-digit reference number given to periodical publications, used in a scheme analogous to the ISBN system.

Journalist A person who writes for a journal, newspaper, periodical, and so on, as distinct from authoring books.

Layout The overall appearance of a script or a printed page.

Libel A printed or broadcast malicious and defamatory statement.

Literary agent A person who acts on behalf of an author in his dealings with publishers, offering his work and negotiating the contracts for work the agent places. Agents always work on commission, usually 10-15 per cent. They don't make any money from your work till you do.

Mainstream fiction A term applied to literary subjects that are traditional or current, as distinct from category or genre fiction.

Market study The analytical study of the author's possible points of sale.

Matter Either manuscript or other copy which is to be printed, or type that is composed for printing.

Media Sources of information, such as newspapers, magazines, radio, TV and so on. (Plural of medium, that is, 'medium of communication'.)

Multiple submissions The sending of the same ms to more than one publisher at a time. In general, this is not an acceptable practice.

Novel A fictional story written in prose, of any length but not usually less than 50,000 words.

'On spec'/on speculation Usually applied to writing submitted to an editor on a purely speculative basis, that is, not by invitation or commission. Also applied to work sent at an editor's invitation but without any commitment from him to accept the piece.

Outline A sketched-out structure of a piece, showing what it will contain and in what order, but without going into detail. See also **Synopsis**.

Out of print No longer on the publisher's list. That is, no longer available except from libraries or second-hand book dealers.

'Over the transom' American slang for the arrival of unsolicited mss.

PB Abbreviation for 'paperback', a book whose covers are made of paper, card or laminated card.

Photo-journalism Journalism in which the text is of secondary importance to the photographs.

Photo-story script A story told in the form of a sequence of photographs with captions.

Picture agency An organisation which keeps photographs and/or illustrations in store and leases reproduction rights to writers and publishers.

Picture fees 1. Fees paid by an author or publisher for the right to reproduce illustrations in which he does not hold the copyright. 2. Fees paid by a publisher to an author or journalist for the right to reproduce his illustrations.

Picture-story script A story told in a sequence of artist-drawn pictures, with dialogue shown in balloons, and perhaps with supplementary captions.

Plagiarism The use without permission, whether deliberate or accidental, of work in which the copyright is held by someone else.

Plot The storyline, the central thread with which everything else that happens is interwoven.

PLR Public Lending Right. A system of monetary reward for writers, based on the number of times their works are borrowed from public libraries. The award any one writer will receive depends on the book meeting certain conditions and being borrowed a minimum number of times.

Professional journal A publication produced specifically for circulation in a particular profession, for example *The Lancet* (medicine).

Proofs An impression or series of impressions of the typeset matter for checking and correction before the final printing.

Proposal A suggested idea for a book, usually put to the publisher in the form of an initial query ('Would you be interested in . . . ?'), then as a synopsis of the whole work, with a sample chapter or two.

Publisher's reader A person employed by a publisher to evaluate a manuscript and to give the publisher a written summary and report, to help the publisher to assess its potential as a published work.

Readership A collective term applied to the people who habitually read a particular publication.

Reading fee A fee charged by an agent, magazine or publisher to read a submitted ms. Usually refundable in the event of acceptance and publication.

Rights Those parts of an author's copyright which he leases to a publisher as specified in a contract.

Royalty A percentage of the published price of a book payable to the author under the terms of his contract. How much he receives depends on the percentage agreed and on the number of copies sold.

SAE (US **SASE**) Stamped addressed envelope (US self-addressed stamped envelope). An envelope addressed back to the sender, and bearing adequate postage stamps.

'Scissors-and-paste job' A contemptuous term applied to work that consists of material 'lifted' from reference books, encyclopedias, magazines, and so on, rearranged and then passed off as an original piece of writing.

Screenplay A film script that includes cinematic information—for example, camera movements—as well as dialogue.

'Slush-pile' A term applied to the unsolicited mss which accu- mulate in an editorial office. So-called because of the sen- timental and emotional content of a large proportion of these mss.

Small presses Small businesses, often one-person operations, producing publications ranging from duplicated pamphlets to bound books, and of very variable production quality. Seldom profitable, and usually financed by their proprietors and/or other enthusiasts.

Staff-writer (US **staffer**) A writer employed and salaried by a publisher, as distinct from a freelance.

Storyline The sequence of events that keeps the action of a plot moving forward: 'and then . . . and then . . . and next . . .'

Strap/strapline An identification line at the top of a manuscript page.

Submission A manuscript that is sent—submitted—to a publisher, with a view to possible publication.

Subsidiary rights A term usually applied to rights other than UK book publication rights. For example, film and TV rights, foreign language rights, serial rights and so on.

Synopsis A précis or condensed version of the theme and contents of a book, giving a clear outline and breakdown of the proposed text.

Syntax The way in which words or phrases are put together.

Taboos Subjects, words, references, that are not acceptable to certain publications.

Technical writing The writing of company and product manuals, reports, engineering and computing manuals and so on.

Text The body of typeset matter in a book, as distinct from headings, footnotes, illustrations, and such like.

Textbooks Usually applied to books written for the educational market.

Theme The subject of a story, the thread that links the narrative, for example a moral concept—'crime doesn't pay', 'love con- quers all'—or a specific human quality, like courage or greed, self-sacrifice or failure. Not to be confused with the plot.

Trade journal A publication produced for circulation among practitioners and companies in a particular trade or industry, for example *The Bookseller, The Grocer*.

Unsolicited manuscript/unsolicited submission A piece of work sent to a publisher completely without invitation.

Usual terms/usual rates The usual rate of payment which a publication offers to freelance writers.

'Vanity' publishing A term applied to the publication of work on behalf of an author who pays someone else to publish the work for him.

Voucher copy A copy of a single issue of a publication, sent free to a writer whose work appears in that issue, as a courtesy and as evidence (to vouch) that the work has in fact been published.

Word processor (WP) A machine which uses computer logic to accept, store and retrieve material for editing and eventual printing out in typewritten or printed form.

Workshop A group of people meeting to exchange opinions and constructive suggestions on current work, usually under the guidance of a writer/tutor.

Writers' circle A group of people meeting to read, discuss and possibly criticise each other's work. Differs from a workshop in that the work is usually done at home before instead of during the meeting.

Writers' seminar A meeting of writers, usually lasting at least one day, where there are guest speakers, discussions, possibly workshops, and where writers can make contact with other writers, both published and unpublished.

Yearbook A book published annually, reviewing the past year's events and/or updating information.

Associations and Societies Open to Unpublished Writers

Association of Comics Enthusiasts (ACE). For collectors of comics and strip cartoons. ACE issues *Comic Cuts* newsletter/ magazine (eight issues a year, specimen copy £1). Annual subscription £8. Contact Denis Gifford, 80 Silverdale, Sydenham, London SE26 4SJ. Tel: (081) 699 7725.

Association of Little Presses (ALP). New members always welcome. Formed to bring together, inform and assist small presses (these are usually one-or two-person outfits) publishing poetry and other literature. Issues a (roughly) bi-monthly newsletter of information about the world of little presses, giving printing and production tips, sources of stationery supplies, services and so on, *Poetry and Little Press Information* magazine (PALPI), and the current catalogue of *Little Press Books in Print.* Annual subscription £10, which covers all the above. Contact Bob Cobbing, ALP, 89A Petherton Road, London N5 2QT Tel: (071) 226 2657.

British Academy of Songwriters, Composers & Authors (BASCA). (*Note:* 'Authors' in this title refers to authors of lyrics.) Associate membership is available to unpublished songwriters. BASCA offers a comprehensive professional advice and guidance service. Members receive a quarterly information magazine, *BASCA News.* Annual subscription from £16. For full details contact General Secretary Eileen Stow, 34 Hanway Street, London W1P 9DE. Tel: (071) 436 2261.

British Amateur Press Association. Brings together people interested in the various arts and crafts of journalism *as a hobby.* Annual subscription £5. Address: Michaelmas, Cimarron Close, South Woodham Ferrers, Essex CM3 5PB. Tel: (0245) 324059.

The British Fantasy Society (BFS). Covers the fantasy, horror and science fiction fields. Publishes a regular newsletter of information and reviews of books, films and events, and its own magazine *Dark Horizons*, containing fiction and articles; also other magazines of specialist interest in this field. Organises an annual fantasy conference, 'Fantasycon', and the British Fantasy Awards. Membership open to all. Annual subscription from £12 (includes all the BFS magazines). Contact Secretary Di Wathen, 15 Stanley Road, Morden, Surrey SM4 5DE. Tel: (081) 540 9443.

British Science Fiction Association. Publishes a critical journal *Vector*, a review supplement *Paperback Inferno*, and a newsletter, all bi-monthly. *Focus* (three a year) has articles on writing and markets, to encourage new writers. There's also a science fiction information service. Annual subscription £12. Contact the Membership Secretary, Jo Raine, 29 Thornville Road, Hartlepool, Cleveland TS26 8EW.

Bureau of Freelance Photographers (BFP). Membership open to professional and amateur photographers and writers. Offers a monthly newsletter full of factual, verified information on current markets for photographs and photo-journalism, an advisory service, a fee recovery service, and discounts on photographic goods and services. Publishes an annual 250 page BFP *Freelance Photographers' Market Handbook*. All the above are included in the annual membership fee of £32.50. For more details (including a free two-month introductory offer) contact John Tracy, Bureau of Freelance Photographers, Focus House, 497 Green Lanes, London N13 4BP. Tel: (081) 882 3315.

Comedy Writers Association. A non-profit-making club to help new and established comedy writers sell their work. Aims to help and encourage fellow writers, to provide members with regular market information, and to promote comedy writing. There's a monthly market information bulletin, and meetings in various parts of the country (members are encouraged to contact each other), visits to radio and TV studios, rehearsals and programme recordings, a library geared to comedy writing, and an annual working holiday/conference. CWA members work at professional levels, and if you haven't already sold material to radio and/or TV you'll be asked to complete a set of test exercises which will be assessed by the committee. Annual membership fee £40. Contact the President, Ken Rock, 61 Parry Road, Ashmore Park, Wolverhampton, West Midlands WV11 2PS. Tel: (0902) 722729.

The J.T. Edson Appreciation Society. Formed to bring J.T.

and his readers together—'he is a writer who cares'. The society issues a bi-monthly newsletter, discussing J.T.'s books and their characters and answering members' questions about the Old West. There are jokes and puzzles, competitions and a pen-pals section. J.T. Edson takes an active part in the society, and it's informal and friendly. *Please note*: Neither J.T. nor the society can undertake criticism so don't send mss. For details contact the Secretary, Mrs Joan Coulter, J.T. Edson Appreciation Society, PO Box 13, Melton Mowbray, Leics.

Fellowship of Christian Writers. Membership open to 'those who desire to serve Jesus Christ in the realm of writing'. For those interested in all types of writing: novels, children's books, articles, poetry, radio . . . There's a manuscript criticism service, fees by arrangement. Has a countrywide network of writers' groups. Annual subscription £5. Contact Hon. Secretary Janet Hall, Shee-Dy-Vea, 151A Bedford Road, Marston Morteyne, Beds, MK43 0LD. Tel: (0234) 767470.

The Friends of the Arvon Foundation. Active in support of the Arvon Foundation. Issues a regular newsletter of information about events, competitions, writers' markets and literature, and details of current and projected Arvon writers' courses. Membership fee £5 per annum. Contact Hon. Secretary Edna Eglinton, 9 North Street, North Tawton, Devon EX20 2DE. Tel: (0837) 82816.

Guild of International Songwriters & Composers (GISC). Aims to give advice and guidance to its songwriter, composer and home recordist members. Open to amateur as well as professional songwriters. Offers members song assessments, collaboration between lyric writers and composers, information on music publishers' requirements, advice about copyright, contracts, demonstration tapes, presentation and so on. A free quarterly magazine, *Songwriting and Composing*, is issued to members. Annual subscription £20 (UK), £25 (overseas). Contact the Chairman, Roderick G. Jones, Sovereign House, 12 Trewartha Road, Praa Sands, Penzance, Cornwall TR20 9ST. Tel: (0736) 762826; Fax: (0736) 763328. GISC has an associated music publishing company, **First Time Music (Publishing) UK Ltd**, at the same address.

London Screenwriters Workshop. Open to anyone interested in writing for film and TV, and to those working in these and related media. Practical workshops held in London, and out-of-town members can send in scripts for reading and criticism by practising screenwriters. Has members throughout the UK and beyond. Issues a newsletter, and advises members about agents and producers. Annual subscription £15. 1 Greek Street, London W1V 6NQ. Tel: (081) 551 5570. Send a large SAE for full details.

National Poetry Foundation. Offers a bi-annual magazine, *Pause*, appraisal of members' poems, possible publication in *Pause*, possible eventual publication of a book of your poems (at no cost to you), news of competitions and literature, all covered by the annual membership fee of £16. Organises poetry recitals in aid of poetry, with a cast of professional actors and actresses. The proceeds from these events, and the generous sponsorship of Rosemary Arthur, now enable the Foundation to make grants to other poetry magazines and to individual poets. For full details contact the Founder, Johnathon Clifford, 27 Mill Road, Fareham, Hants PO16 0TH. Tel: (0329) 822218.

New Playwrights Trust. Open to all playwrights and others interested in the development of playwriting. Offers comprehensive information services, workshops and a writer/company Link Service. Annual subscription £15 (reductions for unwaged or part-waged). Contact New Playwrights Trust, Whitechapel Library, 77 Whitechapel High Street, London E1 7QX. Tel: (071) 377 5429.

The Penman Club. World-wide membership open to all writers. Membership includes free criticism of mss, general and marketing advice, a free library service (you pay only the postage). Annual membership fee £8.25 (there's a one-off joining fee of £3). Contact the General Secretary, Leonard G. Stubbs FRSA, 175 Pall Mall, Leigh-on-Sea, Essex SS9 1RE. Tel: (0702) 74438.

Player-Playwrights (at St Augustine's Church Hall, Queens Gate, London SW1). A long-established society of amateur and professional writers and actors. Welcomes newcomers to play and television writing. Members' scripts are performed, then discussed. Contact the Secretary, Peter Thompson, 9 Hillfield Park, London N10 3QT. Tel: (081) 883 0371.

The Poetry Book Society. A book club. Subscription covers a quarterly bulletin, a free annual poetry anthology, and the opportunity to buy quality poetry books at discount prices. Annual subscription £21.50. Contact The Poetry Book Society, 21 Earls Court Square, London SW5 9DE. Tel: (071) 244 9792.

The Poetry Society. Membership open to all. Membership fee covers a year's subscription to *Poetry Review Quarterly* and members' information bulletin, advance notification of all Poetry Society events, entitlement to reduced admission charges/concessionary tickets to Literature Festival Council events, access to special offers from the Poetry Society Bookshop, reduced rates for use of the Critical Service (see services, p.167). Fees: London £20, elsewhere in Britain/Ireland £15. Other rates on application. Contact The Poetry Society, 21 Earls Court Square, London SW5 9DE. Tel (071) 373 2551. *Note*: Although the Poetry Society and The Poetry Book Society share an address, they are separate organisations, and should be addressed separately.

The Romantic Novelists' Association. Offers probationary membership to unpublished romantic novelists, conditional on being prepared to submit a full length ms to be considered for the Netta Muskett Award for New Writers. For full details of membership, conditions and how to submit your ms, contact Hon. Sec. Marie Murray, 9 Hillside Road, Southport, Merseyside PR8 4QB.

The Scottish Association of Writers. Groups, clubs and workshops for writers throughout Scotland. Organises conferences, competitions and weekend schools for members. Membership open to any group of writers (no minimum number of writers) forming a club/circle/workshop. Individual postal membership can be arranged. Fees £5 per club plus £1 fee per member. Details from the Secretary, Mrs Beth Thomson, 1D Vicarland Place, Kirkhill, Cambuslang, Glasgow G72 8QE. Tel: (041) 641 7203.

Theatre Writers Union. For all who write for live performance. Has a national branch network, gives legal and professional advice, supplies copies of standard contracts and a regular newsletter. Open to anyone who has written a play, whether performed or not. Subscriptions are related to income from playwriting. Details on request from: Actors Centre, 4 Chenies Street, London WC1E 7EP. Tel: (071) 631 3619.

Services

CRITICISM AND MANUSCRIPT ASSESSMENT SERVICES

The London School of Journalism undertakes the criticism and editing of full-length novels, memoirs, biographies and other literary works. Three forms of criticism are offered:
1. A general report and opinion.
2. A more detailed and constructive criticism with suggested revision.
3. Complete editing of a manuscript.
   The fees will depend on which service you choose. Details from The Secretary, The London School of Journalism, 19 Hertford Street, Park Lane, London W1X 8BB. Tel: (071) 499 8250.

National Poetry Foundation will give appraisals of your poems as part of the benefits of membership, which costs £16 per annum. Contact the Founder, Johnathon Clifford, National Poetry Foundation, 27 Mill Road, Fareham, Hants PO16 0TH. Tel: (0329) 822218.

Oriel Critical Service for Writers (for writers living in Wales only). This service is supported by the Welsh Arts Council. It offers constructive advice based on a close reading of submitted work, and gives rigorous and detailed criticism. For full details of the service and current fees contact Oriel Critical Service, Oriel Bookshop, The Friary, Cardiff CF1 4AA.

The Penman Criticism Service. Membership of the Penman Club entitles you to criticism of mss at no further charge. See page 165.

The Poetry Society Critical Service. Founded by Norman Hidden. Professional experts provide detailed reports on poetry.

For full details, contact The Administrator, Poetry Society Critical Service, 21 Earls Court Square, London SW5 9DE. Tel: (071) 373 7861.

Radio and Television Script Criticism Service: Rosemary Horstmann offers expert criticism and tuition, see Chapter 12. Contact Rosemary Horstmann, 43 Westcombe Park Road, Blackheath, London SE3 7QZ. Tel: (081) 853 4706.

Scriptmate Readers-for-Writers Advisory Service. A personal service on almost every field of writing, offered in two related stages:

1. A reader's report with constructive revision suggestions, sent to you direct from a professional reader selected specifically for you.
2. Reassessment after revision, with advice on where and how to submit your ms to publishers or literary agents.

Scriptmate is *not* a writing school or a literary agency. The Stage One and Stage Two fee is £99.88 including VAT for books up to 350 pages. For full details and current charges, and details of other Scriptmate services, contact Ann Kritzinger, Scriptmate & Booksprint, 20 Shepherds Hill, London N6 5AH. Tel: (071) 490 1344 and (081) 341 7650.

INFORMATION SERVICES AND SOURCES

Book Trust. A marvellous source of information on all things literary: prizes, publications, exhibitions, readings, books in print and so on. For details of all Book Trust services, send an SAE (6½ x 9ins) to The Publicity Officer, Book Trust, Book House, 45 East Hill, London SW18 2QZ. Tel: (081) 870 9055/8.

British Library Newspaper Library. Colindale Avenue, London NW9 5HE. Tel: (071) 636 1544.

Freelance Press Services are agents for Writer's Digest Books (USA), and for *Writer's Digest* and *The Writer* American magazines. They'll send a book catalogue on request. They also publish *Freelance Market News*, a monthly bulletin of market information and news for writers, and organise occasional writers' seminars. For details of their services, contact Managing Editor Arthur Waite, Freelance Press Services, Cumberland House, Lissadel Street, Salford, Manchester M6 6GG. Tel: (061) 745 8850.

French's Theatre Bookshop (Samuel French Ltd) is an excellent source of books and cassettes on all the media and performing arts, including writing. They'll send you lists on request (it helps if you specify your area(s) of interest). French's operate a comprehensive mail order service. Details from French's Theatre Bookshop, 52 Fitzroy Street, London W1P 6JR. Tel: (071) 387 9373.

Greeting Card and Calendar Association is a professional association of greeting card companies. Where possible they'll try to help with individual enquiries about their members' requirements. Contact The Information Officer, Greeting Card and Calendar Association, 6 Wimpole Street, London W1M 8AS. Tel: (071) 637 7692.

The Association's bi-monthly magazine, *Greetings*, is available to anyone who wants to subscribe to it. It's an ideal source of information about current greeting card and calendar production, new companies, products and so on. Annual subscription £16. Contact Haymarket Publishing, 38-42 Hampton Road, Teddington, Middlesex TW11 0JE. Tel: (081) 977 8787.

Literary research service: All subjects, but specialising in biography, and police and criminal history (including associated political and social effects). Other literary services, including 'ghosting', are available. Contact Rod Richards, 'Tracking Line', 23 Spearhill, Lichfield, Staffs WS14 9UD. Tel: (0543) 254748.

Network Scotland Ltd, an information broker delivering high quality information on a broad range of subjects. A leaflet detailing services can be obtained on request. For general information contact Network Scotland Ltd, 74 Victoria Crescent Road, Glasgow G12 9JQ. Tel: (041) 357 1774. For information about education and training services, contact the Senior Information Officer, Network Scotland Ltd, Education and Training Section, Unit 11a, Anderston Cross Centre, Glasgow G2 7PH. Tel: (041) 225 5859.

NIACE (The National Institute of Adult Continuing Education, England and Wales) publishes (twice a year) the booklet *Residential Short Courses*, £2.50 post paid. Contact NIACE, 19b De Montfort Street, Leicester LE1 7GE. Tel: (0533) 551451.

Oriel, The Welsh Arts Council's Bookshop, offers a variety of services to writers and small and new publishers; as well as the Writers' Critical Service for writers living in Wales, there's a regular programme of literary events, an *ad hoc* advice service to small and new publishers looking for ways to market their publications, a regularly updated address list of small presses and little magazines, and a mail order service selling books about books and writing. Details of all Oriel's services and their book lists from Peter Finch, Oriel Bookshop, The Friary, Cardiff CF1 4AA.

Photographic agency: Popperfoto, Paul Popper Limited, 24 Bride Lane, Fleet Street, London EC4Y 8DR. Tel: (071) 353 9665/6.

LITERARY AGENTS

Diane Burston, Literary Agent, 46 Cromwell Avenue, Highgate, London N6 5HL. Tel: (081) 340 6130.

Dorian Literary Agency (Dorothy Lumley), Bay Tree House, 10 Nut Bush Lane, Chelston, Devon TQ2 6RZ. Tel: (0803) 605948.

Gregory & Radice Authors' Agents, Riverside Studios, Crisp Road, Hammersmith, London W6 9RL. Tel: (081) 741 3646; Fax: (081) 846 9039.

PRINTING/PUBLISHING SERVICES

Deanhouse Limited, Publishers and print originators (academic material only)., Contact Roland P. Seymour, Deanhouse Limited, The Mews House, Court Walk, Betley, Near Crewe, Cheshire CW3 9DP. Tel: (0270) 820053.

Scriptmate, editorial services and short-run digitally printed paperbacks. Scriptmate offers a range of services which are worth looking at in detail. For more information contact Ann Kritzinger, Scriptmate, 20 Shepherds Hill, London N6 5AH. Tel: (071) 490 1344 and (081) 341 7650.

WRITERS' ACCOMMODATION SERVICE

The London Writing Rooms, Farringdon House, 105-107 Farringdon Road, Clerkenwell, London EC1R 3BT. Tel: (071) 278 7879. Rooms available for writers to rent as places of work.

CORRESPONDENCE COURSES

The Academy of Children's Writers Ltd, 3 Regal Lane, Soham, Ely, Cambridgeshire CB7 5BA. Tel: (0353) 721899.

Children's Authorship. Course details from Children's Features, Freelance Press Services, Cumberland House, Lissadel Street, Salford, Manchester M6 6GG. Tel: (061) 745 8850.

London School of Journalism, 19 Hertford Street, Park Lane, London W1Y 8BB. Tel: (071) 499 8250.

Tutortex Services, 55 Lightburn Avenue, Ulverston, Cumbria LA12 0DL. Tel: (0229) 56333. (Technical writing only.)

'Written By'. Full course or shorter, specialised courses. Details from 'Written By' 2 Brook Farm Road, Cobham, Surrey KT11 3AX. Tel: (0932) 866189 or (081) 644 5297.

POSTAL WORKSHOPS

Directory of Postal Workshops. Lists countrywide writing workshops conducted by post. Contact Mrs Catherine M. Gill, Drakemyre Croft, Cairnorrie, Methlick, Ellon, Aberdeenshire AB41 0JN. (£1 post paid).

SEMINARS AND RESIDENTIAL COURSES

The Arvon Foundation runs residential courses at two centres in England: Lumb Bank, Heptonstall, Hebden Bridge, West Yorkshire HX7 6DF. Tel: (070 681) 6582. And Totleigh Barton, Sheepwash, Devon EX21 5NS.

London Media Workshops run seminars (between one and five days) on writing for radio, TV, video and the press. Contact Mrs Sylvia Angel, London Media Workshops, 101 King's Drive, Gravesend, Kent DA12 5BQ. Tel: (0474) 64676.

Caerleon Writers' Holiday. An annual week-long conference, packed with lectures, seminars, workshops and so on. Usually held in July. Full details and booking form from D.L. Anne Hobbs, 30 Pant Road, Newport, Gwent NP9 5PR. Tel and fax: (0633) 854976.

Scarborough Writers' Weekend. Held annually, usually in April. Top speakers, workshops, discussion groups. Details from the Secretary, Audrey Wilson, 7 Osgodby Close, Osgodby, Scarborough, North Yorkshire YO11 3JW. (Enclose an SAE.)

Swanwick Writers' Summer School. An annual six-day event, usually held in August. Usually over-subscribed, so early booking is advisable. Contact the Secretary, Mrs Philippa Boland, The Red House, Marden Hill, Crowborough, Sussex TN6 1XN. (*Note:* Swanwick is in Derbyshire.)

See also **NIACE** directory of residential courses (page 169).

More useful addresses

PROFESSIONAL ASSOCIATIONS

The Arts Council of Great Britain, 105 Piccadilly, London WIV 0AU. Tel: (071) 629 9495.

British Broadcasting Corporation (BBC), Broadcasting House, Portland Place, London W1A 1AA. Tel: (071) 580 4468.

National Council for the Training of Journalists (NCTJ), Carlton House, Hemnall, Epping, Essex CM16 4NL. Tel: (0378) 72395.

National Union of Journalists (NUJ), Acorn House, 314 Gray's Inn Road, London WC1X 8DP. Tel: (071) 278 7916.

The Newspaper Society Training Department, Whitefriars House, Carmelite Street, London EC4Y 0BL. Tel: (071) 583 3311.

The Society of Authors, 84 Drayton Gardens, London SW10 9SB. Tel: (071) 373 6642.

Workers' Educational Association (WEA), National Office, Temple House, 9 Upper Berkeley Street, London W1H 8BY.

The Writers' Guild of Great Britain, 430 Edgware Road, London W2 1EH. Tel: (071) 723 8074.

PUBLISHERS MENTIONED IN THE TEXT

Allison & Busby, Virgin Publishing Ltd, 338 Ladbroke Grove, London W10 5AH. Tel: (081) 968 7554; Fax: (081) 968 0929.

Andersen Press Ltd, 20 Vauxhall Bridge Road, London SW1V 2SA. Tel: (071) 973 9720; Fax: (071) 233 6263.

Argus Books, Argus House, Boundary Way, Hemel Hempstead, Herts HP2 7ST. Tel: (0442) 66551; Fax: (0442) 66998.

Bantam Press—an imprint of **Transworld Publishers Ltd.**

B.T. Batsford Ltd, 4 Fitzhardinge Street, London W1H 0AH. Tel: (071) 486 8484; Fax: (071) 487 4296.

BBC Books, 80 Wood Lane, London W12 0TT. Tel: (081) 576 2000; Fax: (081) 749 8766.

A. & C. Black (Publishers) Ltd, 35 Bedford Row, London WC1R 4JH. Tel: (071) 242 0946; Fax: (071) 831 8478.

Blackie Children's Books, 7 Leicester Place, London WC2H 7BP. Tel: (071) 734 7521; Fax: (071) 437 0498.

Blackwell Publishers, 108 Cowley Road, Oxford OX4 1JF. Tel: (0865) 791100; Fax: (0865) 791347.

Blandford Publishing Ltd, Villiers House, 41-47 Strand, London WC2N 5JE. Tel: (071) 839 4900; Fax: (071) 839 1804.

Blueprint Publishing, Chapman & Hall, 206 Boundary Row, London SE1 8HN. Tel: (071) 865 0066; Fax: (071) 522 9623.

Marion Boyars Publishers Ltd, 24 Lacy Road, London SW15 1NL. Tel: (081) 788 9522; Fax: (081) 789 8122.

Brimax Books Ltd, 4-5 Studlands Park Industrial Estate, Exning Road, Newmarket, Suffolk CB8 7AU. Tel: (0638) 664611; Fax (0638) 665220.

Jonathan Cape Ltd, Random Century House, 20 Vauxhall Bridge Road, London SW1V 2SA. Tel: (071) 973 9730; Fax: (071) 233 6117.

Cassell plc, Villiers House, 41-47 Strand, London WC2N 5JE. Tel: (071) 839 4900; Fax: (071) 839 1804.

Century Publishing Ltd, Random Century House, 20 Vauxhall Bridge Road, London SW1V 2SA. Tel: (071) 973 9670; Fax: (071) 233 6125.

W. & R. Chambers Ltd, 43-45 Annandale Street, Edinburgh EH7 4AZ. Tel: (031) 557 4571; Fax: (031) 557 2936.

Constable & Co Ltd, 3 The Lanchesters, 162 Fulham Palace Road, W6 9ER. Tel: (081) 741 3663; Fax: (081) 748 7562.

Corgi—an imprint of **Transworld Publishers Ltd.**

Darton, Longman & Todd Ltd, 89 Lillie Road, London SW6 1UD. Tel: (071) 385-2341; Fax (071) 381 4556.

David & Charles plc, Brunel House, Newton Abbot, Devon TQ12 4PU. Tel: (0626) 61121; Fax: (0626) 64463.

Dorling Kindersley Ltd, 9 Henrietta Street, London WC2E 8PS. Tel: (071) 836 5411; Fax: (071) 836 7570.

Elm Tree Books—an imprint of **Hamish Hamilton Ltd.**

Faber & Faber Ltd, 3 Queen Square, London WC1N 3AU. Tel: (071) 465 0045; Fax: (071) 465 0034.

Samuel French Ltd, 52 Fitzroy Street, London W1P 6JR. Tel: (071) 387 9373; Fax: (071) 387 2161. (Plays only.)

Victor Gollancz Ltd, 14 Henrietta Street, London WC2E 8QJ. Tel: (071) 836 2006; Fax: (071) 379 0934.

Grafton Books Ltd, 77-85 Fulham Palace Road, London W6 8JB. Tel: (081) 741 7070; Fax: (081) 307 4440.

Robert Hale Ltd, Clerkenwell House, 45-47 Clerkenwell Green, London EC1R 0HT. Tel: (071) 251 2661; Fax: (071) 490 4958.

Hamish Hamilton Ltd, 27 Wrights Lane, London W8 5TZ. Tel: (071) 938 3388; Fax: (071) 937 8704.

HarperCollins Publishers, 77-85 Fulham Palace Road, London W6 8JB. Tel: (081) 741 7070; Fax: (081) 307 4440.

Harrap Publishing Group Ltd, Chelsea House, 26 Market Square, Bromley, Kent BR1 1NA. Tel: (081) 313 3484; Fax: (081) 313 0702.

Headline Book Publishing, Headline House, 79 Great Titchfield Street, London W1P 7FN. Tel: (071) 631 1687; Fax: (071) 631 1958.

William Heinemann Ltd, Michelin House, 81 Fulham Road, London SW3 6RB. Tel: (071) 581 9393; Fax: (071) 589 8437.

Hodder & Stoughton Ltd, 47 Bedford Square, London WC1B 3DP. Tel: (071) 636 9851; Fax (071) 631 5248.

How To Books Ltd, Plymbridge House, Estover Road, Plymouth, Devon PL6 7PZ. Tel: (0752) 735251; Fax: (0752) 695699.

Kingfisher Books, Elsley House, 24-30 Great Titchfield Street, London W1P 7AD. Tel: (071) 631 0878; Fax: (071) 323 4694.

Kogan Page Ltd, 120 Pentonville Road, London N1 9JN. Tel: (071) 278 0433; Fax: (071) 837 3768.

Lion Publishing plc, Peter's Way, Sandy Lane West, Oxford OX4 5HG. Tel: (0865) 747550; Fax: (0865) 747568.

Longman Group UK Ltd, Longman House, Burnt Mill, Harlow, Essex CM20 2JE. Tel: (0279) 426721; Fax: (0279) 431059.

Macdonald & Co Ltd, 165 Great Dover Street, London SE1 4YA. Tel: (071) 334 4800; Fax; (071) 334 4905/6.

Macmillan Academic & Professional Ltd, 4 Little Essex Street, London WC2R 3LF. Tel: (071) 836 6633; Fax: (071) 379 4980.

Macmillan Education Ltd, Brunel Road, Houndmills, Basingstoke, Hants RG21 2XS. Tel: (0256) 29242.

Merehurst Ltd, Ferry House, 51-57 Lacy Road, London SW15 1PR. Tel: (081) 780 1177; Fax: (081) 780 1714.

Methuen London, Michelin House, 81 Fulham Road, London SW3 6RB. Tel: (071) 581 9393; Fax: (071) 225 0933.

Mills & Boon Ltd, Eton House, 18-24 Paradise Road, Richmond, Surrey TW9 1SR. Tel: (081) 948 0444; Fax: (081) 940 5899.

Mitchell Beazley Ltd, Michelin House, 81 Fulham Road, London SW3 6RB. Tel: (071) 581 9393; Fax: (071) 584 8268.

Mulholland-Wirral, The Croft, School Avenue, Little Neston, South Wirral L64 4BS. (Telephone unlisted.)

New English Library—an imprint of **Hodder & Stoughton Ltd.**

Northcote House Publishers Ltd, Plymbridge House, Estover Road, Plymouth, Devon PL6 7PZ. Tel: (0752) 735251; Fax: (0752) 695699.

Oxford University Press, Walton Street, Oxford OX2 6DP. Tel: (0865) 56767; Fax: (0865) 56646.

Pan Books Ltd, 18-21 Cavaye Place, London SW10 9PG. Tel: (071) 373 6070; Fax: (071) 370 0746.

Pelham Books, 27 Wrights Lane, London W8 5TZ. Tel: (071) 937 7255; Fax: (071) 937 8704.

Robinson Publishing, 11 Shepherd House, 5 Shepherd Street, London W1Y 7LD. Tel: (071) 493 1064; Fax: (071) 409 7226.

SCM Press Ltd, 26-30 Tottenham Road, London N1 4BZ. Tel: (071) 249 7262/5; Fax: (071) 249 3776.

Severn House Publishers, 35 Manor Road, Wallington, Surrey SM6 0BW. Tel: (081) 773 4161; Fax: (081) 773 4143.

Simon & Schuster Ltd, West Garden Place, Kendal Street, London W2 2AQ. Tel: (071) 724 7577; Fax: (071) 402 0639.

SPCK (Society for Promoting Christian Knowledge), Holy Trinity Church, Marylebone Road, London NW1 4DU. Tel: (071) 387 5282; Fax: (071) 388 2352.

D.C. Thomson & Co Ltd, Albert Square, Dundee DD1 9QJ. Tel: (0382) 23131; Fax: (0382) 22214.

Thorsons, 77-85 Fulham Palace Road, London W6 8JB. Tel: (081) 741 7070; Fax: (081) 307 4440.

Transworld Publishers Ltd, 61-63 Uxbridge Road, London W5 5SA. Tel: (081) 579 2652; Fax: (081) 579 5479.

Viking, 27 Wrights Lane, London W8 5TZ. Tel: (071) 938 2200; Fax: (071) 937 8704.

Virago Press Ltd, 20-23 Mandela Street, Camden Town, London NW1 0HQ. Tel: (071) 383 5150; Fax: (071) 383 4802.

Walker Books Ltd, 87 Vauxhall Walk, London SE11 5HJ. Tel: (071) 793 0909; Fax: (071) 587 1123.

J. Whitaker & Sons Ltd, 12 Dyott Street, London WC1A 1DF. Tel: (071) 836 8911; Fax: (071) 836 2909.

The Women's Press, 34 Great Sutton Street, London EC1V oDX. Tel: (071) 251 3007; Fax: (071) 608 1938.

Writer's Digest Books, 1507 Dana Avenue, Cincinnati, Ohio 45207, USA.

THEATRE COMPANIES

Liverpool Playhouse, Williamson Square, Liverpool L1 1EL. Tel: (051) 709 8478; Fax: (051) 709 7113.

Paines Plough, The Writers Company, Interchange Studios, 15 Wilkin Street, London NW5 3NG. Tel: (071) 284 4483; Fax: (071) 284 4506.

Traverse Theatre, 112 West Bow, Grassmarket, Edinburgh EH1 2HH. Tel: (031) 225 1974; Fax: (031) 225 3308.

GREETING CARD COMPANIES

Graphic Humour, Unit 17, Dudley Court, Manor Walks Centre, Cramlington, Northumberland NE23 6QW. Tel: (0670) 590975; Fax: (0670) 590084.

Hanson-White-Accord, 9th Floor, Wettern House, 56 Dingwall Road, Croydon, Surrey CR0 oXH. Tel: (081) 680 1885; Fax: (081) 760 0093.

Paperlink Ltd, 59-61 Palfrey Place, London SW8 1AR. Tel: (071) 582 8244.

Paper House, Shepherd Road, Gloucester, Glos GL2 6EL. Tel: (0452) 423451; Fax: (0452) 410312.

United Greeting Card Co (UK) Ltd, River Park, Billet Lane, Berkhamsted, Herts HP4 1EL. Tel: (0442) 871381.

OTHER RELEVANT ORGANISATIONS

Aslib, The Association for Information Management, Information House, 20-24 Old Street, London EC1V 9AP. Tel: (071) 253 4488; Fax: (071) 430 0514.

The Association of Authors' Agents, 79 St Martin's Lane, London WC2N 4AA. Tel: (071) 836 4271.

Cartoonists Club of Great Britain. Secretary: Charles Sinclair, 2 Camden Hill, Tunbridge Wells, Kent TN2 4TH. Tel: (0892) 28938.

Crime Writers' Association. Membership open only to published writers of crime fiction or serious works on crime. Associate membership available to publishers, journalists and booksellers specialising in crime literature. Members frequently speak at writers' seminars. PO Box 172, Tring, Herts HP23 5LP.

Legal Deposit Office, The British Library, Boston Spa, West Yorkshire LS23 7BY. Tel: (0937) 546267; Fax: (0937) 546 586.

Public Lending Right Office, Bayheath House, Prince Regent Street, Stockton-on-Tees, Cleveland TS18 1DF. Tel: (0642) 604699.

Scottish Arts Council, 12 Manor Place, Edinburgh EH3 7DD. Tel: (031) 226 6051.

Society of Civil Service Authors. Secretary: Mrs J. M. Hykin, 8 Bawtree Close, Sutton, Surrey SM2 5LQ.

Society of Freelance Editors and Proofreaders. Secretary: Jane Sugarman, 16 Brenthouse Road, London E9 6QG. Tel: (081) 986 4868.

Society of Indexers. Secretary: Mrs. H.C. Troughton, 16 Green Road, Birchington, Kent CT7 9JZ. Tel: (0843) 41115.

Society of Women Writers and Journalists. Secretary: Jean Hawkes, 110 Whitehall Road, Chingford, London E4 6DW.

Welsh Arts Council, Museum Place, Cardiff CF1 3NX. Tel: (0222) 394711; Fax: (0222) 221447.

Welsh Books Council/Cyngor Llyfrau, Cymraeg, Castell Brychan, Aberystwyth, Dyfed SY23 2JB. Tel: (0970) 624151; Fax: (0970) 625385.

Further reading

BOOKS FOR WRITERS

Joan Aiken, *The Way to Write for Children* (Elm Tree, 1982), pb £6.95.

William Ash, *The Way to Write Radio Drama* (Elm Tree, 1986), pb £6.95.

Brad Ashton, *How to Write Comedy* (Elm Tree, 1983), pb £6.95.

Donna Baker, *How to Write Stories for Magazines* (Allison & Busby, 1986), pb £6.99.

Jill Baker, *Copy Prep* (Blueprint, 1987), hb £14.95.

Michael Baldwin, *The Way to Write Short Stories* (Elm Tree, 1986), pb £6.95.

Michael Barnard, *Magazine and Journal Production* (Blueprint, 1986), hb £19.95.

Julian Birkett, *Word Power—A Guide to Creative Writing* (A. & C. Black, 1983), pb £5.95.

Lawrence Block, *Writing the Novel from Plot to Print* (Writer's Digest Books, 1979), pb £6.95.

Anthony Blond, *The Book Book* (Jonathan Cape, 1985), hb £9.95.

John Braine, *Writing a Novel* (Methuen, 1974), pb £6.95.

Dorothea Brande, *Becoming a Writer* (Papermac, first published 1934), pb £3.95.

William Brohaugh, *Professional Etiquette for Writers* (Writer's Digest Books, 1986), hb $9.95.*

Stewart Bronfield, *Writing for Film and Television* (Simon & Schuster, 1986), pb £5.95.

Morag Campbell, *Writing About Travel* (A. & C. Black, 1989), pb £6.99.

Orson Scott Card, *Characters & Viewpoint*, (Robinson Writer's Workshop, 1990), pb £5.99.

Alison Chisholm, *How to Write Poetry* (Allison & Busby, 1992), pb £6.99.

Stephen Citron, *Songwriting* (Hodder & Stoughton, 1987), hb £14.95.

Giles N. Clark, *Inside Book Publishing* (Blueprint, 1988), hb £12.95.

Oscar Collier with Frances Spatz Leighton, *How to Write and Sell Your First Novel* (Writer's Digest Books, 1986), pb $12.95.*

Lisa Collier Cool, *How to Sell Every Magazine Article You Write* (Writer's Digest Books, 1986), hb $14.95.*

Alastair Crompton, *The Craft of Copywriting* (Century Hutchinson, 1987), pb £6.95.

Alastair Crompton, *Do Your Own Advertising* (Century Hutchinson, 1987), pb £6.95.

Anthony Davis, *Magazine Journalism Today* (Heinemann Professional Publishing, 1988), pb £12.95.

Sheila Davis, *The Craft of Lyric Writing* (Writer's Digest Books, 1986), hb £18.95.*

Ansen Dibell, *Plot* (Robinson Writer's Workshop, 1990), pb £5.99.

Jill Dick, *Freelance Writing for Newspapers* (A. & C. Black, 1991), pb £9.99.

Dianne Doubtfire, *The Craft of Novel-Writing* (Allison & Busby, 1978), pb £4.99.

Christopher Evans, *Writing Science Fiction* (A. & C. Black, 1988), pb £4.95.

George Evans & Vince Powell, *Get Writing* (BBC Books, 1990), pb £4.99.

Hilary Evans, *The Art of Picture Research* (David & Charles, 1979), hb £12.50. (£13.50 incl. p&p from Mary Evans Picture Library, 1 Tranquil Vale, Blackheath, London SE3 oBU. Tel: (081) 318 0034.)

John Fairfax and John Moat, *The Way to Write* (Elm Tree, 1981), pb £6.95.

Peter Finch, *How to Publish Your Poetry* (Allison & Busby, 1988), £6.99.

J.A. Fletcher & D.F. Gowing, *The Business Guide to Effective Writing* (Kogan Page, revised ed. 1987), pb £6.95.

Tom Gallacher, *The Way to Write for the Stage* (Elm Tree, 1988), pb £6.95.

Dilys Gater, *How to Write a Play* (Allison & Busby, 1991), £4.99.

William Gentz and Lee Roddy, *Writing to Inspire* (Writer's Digest Books, 1986), pb $14.95.*

Phillippa Giles and Vicky Licorish, Eds., *Debut on Two* (BBC Books, 1990), pb £4.99.

Fay Goldie, *How to Write Stories and Novels that Sell* (Malvern, 1986), pb £3.95.

Fay Goldie, *Successful Freelance Journalism* (Oxford University Press, 1984), pb £4.95.

Ray Hammond, *The Writer and the Word Processor* (Coronet, 1987), pb £3.95.

Brendan Hennessy, *Writing Feature Articles* (Heinemann Professional Publishing, 1989), pb £12.95.

Patricia Highsmith, *Plotting and Writing Suspense Fiction* (Poplar Press, 1983), pb £4.95.

John Hines, *The Way to Write Magazine Articles* (Elm Tree), pb £5.95.

Rosemary Horstmann, *Writing for Radio*, 2nd Ed. (A. & C. Black, 1991), pb £6.99.

Raymond Hull, *How to Write 'How-To' Books and Articles* (Writer's Digest Books, 1981), pb $8.95.*

H.R.F. Keating, *Writing Crime Fiction* (A. & C. Black, 1986), pb £4.95.

Gerald Kelsey, *Writing for Television*, (A. & C. Black), pb £6.99.

Paddy Kitchen, *The Way to Write Novels* (Elm Tree, 1983), pb £6.95.

Tessa Krailing, *How to Write for Children* (Allison & Busby, 1988), pb £6.99.

Michael Legat, *An Author's Guide to Publishing* 2nd edn. (Robert Hale, 1991), £6.95.

Michael Legat, *How to Write Historical Novels* (Allison & Busby), pb £4.99.

Michael Legat, *Writing for Pleasure and Profit* (Robert Hale, 1986), pb £4.95.

Claudia Lewis, *Writing for Young Children* (Poplar Press, revised edn. 1984), pb £4.95.

Ian Linton, *Writing for a Living* (Kogan Page, 2nd edn. 1988), pb £5.95.

Yvonne MacManus, *You Can Write a Romance and Get it Published!* (Severn House, 1983), hb £5.95.

Rhona Martin, *Writing Historical Fiction* (A. & C. Black, 1988), pb £4.95.

Alan McKenzie, *How to Draw and Sell Comic Strips* (Macdonald Orbis, 1988), hb £12.95.

William Miller, *Screenwriting for Narrative Film and Television* (Harrap Columbus, 1988), pb £7.95.

John Morrison, *Freelancing for Magazines* (Bureau of Freelance Photographers, 1991), hb £12.95.

Harry Mulholland, *Guide to Self-Publishing—The A-Z of Getting Yourself into Print* (Mulholland-Wirral, 1984), pb £7.70 (incl p&p) direct from the publisher—see p. 175.

Lynette Owen, *Selling Rights* (Blueprint 1991), hb £19.95.

Dan Poynter & Mindy Bingham, *Is there a book inside you?* (Exley, 1986), pb £6.95.

Gary Provost, *Make Every Word Count* (Writer's Digest Books, 1980), pb $7.95.*

Kit Reed, *Revision*, (Robinson Writer's Workshop, 1991), pb £5.99.

Philip Davies Roberts, *How Poetry Works* (Pelican, 1986), pb £3.95.

Geoffrey Rogers, *Editing for Print* (Macdonald, 1986), hb £9.95.

Kit Sadgrove, *Writing to Sell—The Complete Guide to Copywriting for Business* (Robert Hale, 1991), hb £14.95.

Larry Sandman (Ed.), *A Guide to Greeting Card Writing* (Writer's Digest Books, 1980), pb $8.95.*

Jean Saunders, *The Craft of Writing Romance* (Allison & Busby, 1986), pb £6.99.

Jean Saunders, *Writing Step by Step* (Allison & Busby, 1988), pb £6.99.

Lew Schwartz, *The Craft of Writing TV Comedy* (Allison & Busby), pb £4.99.

William Smethurst, *How to Write for Television* (How To Books, 1992), pb £8.99.

Ian Stewart, *The Business Writing Workbook* (Kogan Page, 1987), pb £4.95.

Julian Symons, *Bloody Murder* (Penguin, revised edn. 1985), pb £3.95.

Liz Taylor, *The Writing Business* (Severn House, 1985), pb £3.95.

Felicity Trotman, *How to Write and Illustrate Children's Books* (Macdonald Orbis, 1988), hb £12.95.

Lewis Turco, *Dialogue*, (Robinson Writer's Workshop, 1991), pb £5.99.

Jenny Vaughan, *Getting into Print* (Bedford Square Press, 1988), pb £4.95.

Gordon Wells, *The Book Writer's Handbook*, revised edn. (Allison & Busby, 1991), pb £6.99.

Gordon Wells, *The Craft of Writing Articles* (Allison & Busby, 1983), pb £6.99.
Gordon Wells, *The Magazine Writer's Handbook*, 4th edn. (Allison & Busby, 1992), £4.99.
Gordon Wells, *Photography for Article Writers* (Allison & Busby, 1991), pb £4.99.
Gordon Wells, *The Successful Author's Handbook* (Papermac), £7.99.
Gordon Wells, *Writers' Questions Answered* (Allison & Busby, 1986), pb £6.99.
Neil Wenborn, *How to Get Published* (Hamlyn, 1990), pb £2.50.
Phyllis Whitney, *Guide to Fiction Writing* (Poplar Press, 1984), pb £4.95.
Mary Wibberley, *To Writers With Love* (Buchan & Enright, 2nd edn. 1987), pb £4.95.
David Silwyn Williams, *How to Write for Teenagers* (Allison & Busby), pb £4.99.
Writing for the BBC (BBC Publications), pb £3.95.

Note: For all **Poplar Press** titles, contact David & Charles.

* The prices of the American Writer's Digest Books listed are given in US dollars, to give you an idea of their cost. Many of these books are now available through UK bookshops from Harrap Publishers. Freelance Press Services can supply them by mail order, or you can buy them direct from America from Writer's Digest Books, 1507 Dana Avenue, Cincinnati, Ohio 45207, USA.

MAGAZINES AND NEWSPAPERS MENTIONED IN THE TEXT

Alfred Hitchcock's Mystery Magazine, 380 Lexington Avenue, New York NY.
Annabel, The Beano, Beezer-Topper, The Dandy, Jackie, My Weekly, People's Friend, Twinkle and *Victor* are all published by D.C. Thomson & Co. Ltd., Albert Square, Dundee DD1 9QJ. Tel: (0382) 23131. Fax: (0382) 22214.
Bella, Shirley House, 25-27 Camden Road, London NW1 9LL. Tel: (071) 284 0909. Fax: (071) 485 3774.
Best, Portland House, Stag Place, London SW1E 5AU. Tel: (071) 245 8700. Fax: (071) 245 8825.
Canal and Riverboat, Stanley House, 9 West Street, Epsom, Surrey KT18 7RL. Tel: (0372) 741411. Fax: (0372) 744493.

Catholic Herald, Lamb's Passage, Bunhill Row, London EC1Y 8TQ. Tel: (071) 588 3101/5. Fax: (071) 256 9728.

Christian Herald, Herald House, 96 Dominion Road, Worthing, West Sussex BN14 8JP. Tel: (0903) 821082. Fax: (0903) 821081.

Church Times, 33 Upper Street, London N1 6PN. Tel: (071) 359 4570. Fax: (071) 226 3073.

Darts World, World Magazines Ltd, 2 Park Lane, Croydon, Surrey CR9 1HA. Tel: (081) 681 2837. Fax: (081) 688 5159.

Ellery Queen's Mystery Magazine, Davis Publications Inc, 380 Lexington Avenue, New York NY.

Jewish Chronicle, 25 Furnival Street, London EC4A 1JT. Tel: (071) 405 9252. Fax: (071) 405 9040.

Jewish Telegraph, Telegraph House, Bury Old Road, Prestwich, Manchester M25 8HH. Tel: (061) 740 9321. Fax: (061) 740 9325.

The Lady, 39-40 Bedford Street, Strand, London WC2E 9ER. Tel: (071) 379 4717. Fax: (071) 497 2137.

Me, 57-59 Long Acre, London WC2E 9JL. Tel: (071) 836 0519. Fax: (071) 497 2364.

Practical Caring, Stanley House, 9 West Street, Epsom, Surrey KT18 7RL. Tel: (0372) 741411.

Practical Photography, EMAP, Bushfield House, Orton Centre, Peterborough PE2 0UW. Tel: (0733) 237111.

Private Eye, 6 Carlisle Street, London W1V 5RG. Tel: (071) 437 4017. Fax: (071) 437 0705.

Snap, Walker Books Ltd, 87 Vauxhall Walk, London SE11 5HJ. Tel: (071) 793 0909. Fax: (071) 587 1123.

The Stage and Television Today, Stage House, 47 Bermondsey Street, London SE1 3XT. Tel: (071) 403 1818.

The Tablet, 48 Great Peter Street, London SW1P 2HB. Tel: (071) 222 7462. Fax: (071) 222 4967.

Take a Break, Shirley House, 25-27 Camden Road, London NW1 9LL. Tel: (071) 284 0909. Fax: (071) 482 2777.

Woman's Realm, IPC Magazines Ltd., King's Reach Tower, Stamford Street, London SE1 9LS. Tel: (071) 261 5000.

PUBLICATIONS OF PARTICULAR INTEREST TO NEW WRITERS

Acumen, editor Patricia Oxley, 6 The Mount, Higher Furzeham, Brixham, Devon TQ5 8QY. Current subscription rates on request.

The Author, editor Derek Parker. The official magazine of **The Society of Authors**. Available to non-members on subscription. Current rates from the Publications Department, The Society of Authors, 84 Drayton Gardens, London SW10 9SB. Tel: (071) 373 6642.

Book and Magazine Collector, editor John Dean. Monthly from newsagents or by subscription. Current rates on request from Book and Magazine Collector, 43-45 St Mary's Road, Ealing, London W5 5RQ. Tel: (081) 579 1082.

The Bookseller, 'the organ of the book trade', editor Louis Baum. Weekly, to order from newsagents or on subscription. Current rates from The Bookseller, 12 Dyott Street, London WC1A 1DF. Tel: (071) 836 8911. Fax: (071) 836 6381.

Envoi (poetry only), editor Roger Elkin. Three issues per year, UK subscription £9. Overseas rates on application from Envoi, 44 Rudyard Road, Biddulph Moor, Stoke-on-Trent, Staffs ST8 7JN. Tel: (0782) 517892.

First Time (poetry only) editor Josephine Austin. Two issues a year. Current subscription rates from Josephine Austin, Burdett Cottage, 4 Burdett Place, George Street, Old Town, Hastings, East Sussex TN34 3ED.

Freelance Market News, editor Mrs Saundrea Williams. Monthly (except August). Current subscription rates from Mrs Williams, Freelance Market News, Cumberland House, Lissadel Street, Salford, Manchester M6 6GG. Tel: (061) 745 8850.

Freelance Writing & Photography, editor John T. Wilson. Quarterly information/advice magazine for writers. Current rates from Freelance Writing & Photography, Tregeraint House, Zennor, St Ives, Cornwall TR26 3DB. Tel: (0736) 797061. Fax: (0736) 797061.

Greetings, the magazine of The Greeting Card & Calendar Association, editor Terri Mousley. Bi-monthly, subscription £15 per annum from Haymarket Publishing, 38-42 Hampton Road, Teddington, Middlesex, TW11 0JE. Tel: (081) 943 5000. Fax: (081) 943 5658.

Interzone, editor David Pringle. Science fiction and fantasy magazine. Monthly. Available from newsagents or on subscription (UK £26, overseas £32). 217 Preston Drove, Brighton BN1 6FL.

Million, editor David Pringle. A recently launched magazine *about* popular fiction. Includes articles about and interviews with popular authors, discussing their work (often with insights into how they write). Bi-monthly, subscription UK £12, Overseas £15. Address as for *Interzone*.

Outposts Poetry Quarterly, editor Roland John. Subscription: £10 (UK), £13 elsewhere. 22 Whitewell Road, Frome, Somerset BA11 4EL.

Publishing News, editor Fred Newman, 43 Museum Street, London WC1A 1LY. Tel: (071) 404 0304. Fax: (071) 242 0762.

Quartos magazine for writers, editor Suzanne Riley. Bi-monthly, subscription £12 per annum. Address: BCM Writer, 27 Old Gloucester Street, London WC1N 3XX. Tel: (0559) 371108.

Stand Magazine, editors Jon Silkin and Lorna Tracy. Quarterly, subscription £9.95. 179 Wingrove Road, Newcastle upon Tyne NE4 9DA. Tel: (091) 273 3280.

Tees Valley Writer, editor Derek Gregory. Current subscription rates on application. 57 The Avenue, Linthorpe, Middlesbrough, Cleveland TS5 6QU. Tel: (0642) 819102.

Writers' Monthly, editor Shirley Kelly. Subscription £33.50 per annum. 29 Turnpike Lane, London N8 0EP. Tel: (081) 342 8879. Fax: (081) 347 8847.

Writers News, editor Richard Bell. Monthly, subscription £34.90 per annum. PO Box 4, Nairn IV12 4HU, Scotland. Tel: (0667) 54441. Fax: (0667) 54401.

The Writers' Newsletter, editor Patrick Campbell. The official magazine of **The Writers' Guild of Great Britain**. Ten issues per annum. Available to non-members on subscription. Current rates on request from The Writers' Guild of Great Britain, 430 Edgware Road, London W2 1EH. Tel: (071) 723 8074.

Writers' Own Magazine, editor Mrs Eileen M. Pickering. Quarterly, subscription UK £6, overseas £8. Single copy £1.50 (overseas £2). 121 Highbury Grove, Clapham, Bedford MK41 6DU. Tel: (0234) 365982.

The Writers' Rostrum, editor Jenny Chaplin. SAE for current subscription rates. 14 Ardbeg Road, Rothesay, Bute PA20 0NJ, Scotland.

Cassette
'And then he kissed her . . .' £4.95 post paid from Mills & Boon Ltd, Reader Service, PO Box 236, Thornton Road, Croydon, Surrey CR9.

American magazines

The Writer, monthly. Introductory rates offered to new subscribers (in 1991, $10 plus £8 overseas charge for five issues. Usual subscription rates $27 per annum plus $8 overseas charge.) For details of current subs and offers, send an IRC to *The Writer Inc*, 120 Boylston Street, Boston, MA 02116 4615.

Writer's Digest, monthly. Like *The Writer* (above) offers special rates to new subscribers. (1991 rate: $21 per annum plus $4 overseas charge.) *Writer's Digest*, 1507 Dana Avenue, Cincinnati, Ohio 45207.

RECOMMENDED REFERENCE BOOKS

Chambers Twentieth Century Dictionary (1988 edn.), £18.95.

Dictionary of Literary Terms, Martin Gray, (Longman York Handbooks 1984), pb £2.95.

The Oxford Dictionary for Writers and Editors (Clarendon/OUP 1991), hb £8.95.

Pears Cyclopedia (Pelham Books, annual), hb £10.95.

Penguin Dictionary of Historical Slang, ed Eric Partridge (Penguin 1973), pb £7.95.

Research for Writers, Ann Hoffmann (A. & C. Black, 1986), pb £6.95.

Roget's Thesaurus, various editions available.

Spell Well, compiled by Kirkpatrick and Schwartz (Chambers 1980), hb £2.95.

Type it Yourself, Brenda Rowe (Penguin 1975), pb £2.95.

Whitaker's Almanack (J. Whitaker, annual). Complete edn. £22.50, shorter edn £11.95.

Willing's Press Guide (IPC Business Press, annual), hb about £50.

Write Right!, Jan Venolia (David & Charles 1986), hb £4.95.

Writers' & Artists' Yearbook (A. & C. Black, annual), pb £8.99.

The Writer's Handbook (Macmillan/Pen, annual), pb £9.99.

Writer's Market (USA) (Writer's Digest Books, annual), hb £12.95 from Harrap Publishers.

Consult these in the library
British Books in Print (J. Whitaker).
Cassell's Media Directory (Cassell).

USEFUL BOOKLETS

All Write Now, by Pat Saunders. Journalism for disabled people.

50p plus 24p postage from RADAR (The Royal Association for Disability and Rehabilitation), 25 Mortimer Street, London WIN 8AB. Tel: (071) 637 5400.

Author's Guide. Free on receipt of a first class stamp, from David & Charles Publishers plc, Brunel House, Newton Abbot, Devon TQ12 4PU. Tel: (0626) 61121.

Brief Guide to Self-publishing, by Ann Kritzinger. £2.50 post paid from Scriptmate, 20 Shepherds Hill, London N6 5AH.

Directory of Postal Workshops. £1 post paid from Mrs Catherine M. Gill, Drakemyre Croft, Cairnorrie, Methlick, Ellon, Aberdeenshire AB41 0JN.

Directory of Writers' Circles. £3 post paid from Jill Dick, 'Oldacre', Horderns Park Road, Chapel-en-le-Frith, Derbyshire SK12 6SY. (Please make cheques payable to Laurence Pollinger Ltd).

Guidelines for Educational Writers and *Sell Your Writing.* £1.50 each post paid from the Society of Authors, 84 Drayton Gardens, London SW10 9SB.

Howard MBE. A collection of the late Howard Sergeant's poems, writings and thoughts on poetry and poetry writing, edited by his widow, Jean. £4.80 post paid from the National Poetry Foundation, 27 Mill Road, Fareham, Hants PO16 0TH.

Notes on Radio Drama. Free from the Script Editor (Drama), BBC, Broadcasting House, London W1A 1AA.

The Playscript from Scratch. £2.25 post paid from David Huxley, Haslemere Publications, 16 Haslemere Drive, Cheadle Hulme, Cheadle, Cheshire SK8 6JY. Tel: (061) 485 7484.

Quick Guides to: *Copyright, Protection of Titles, Libel, Translators Specimen Contract, Guidelines for Authors of Medical Books, Permissions, The Small Claims Court, Buying a Word Processor, Income Tax, VAT, Authors' Agents, Your Copyrights after Your Death, Guidelines for Authors of Educational Books, Artistic Works including Photographs.*

£1.50 each post free from The Society of Authors.

Theatre Writing Schemes (brochure) on request from the Drama Director, The Arts Council of Great Britain, 105 Piccadilly, London W1V 0AU.

Index